PSA HISTORIC BUILDINGS REGISTER

HISTORIC BUILDINGS IN THE CARE OF

PROPERTY SERVICES AGENCY OF THE

DEPARTMENT OF THE ENVIRONMENT

VOLUME III   SOUTHERN ENGLAND

Series Editor Alasdair Glass

ARCHITECTURAL SERVICES DIVISION

ISBN 0 86177 084 6

Volume I   Northern and Eastern England
            the Midlands and Wales

Volume II   London

Volume III Southern England

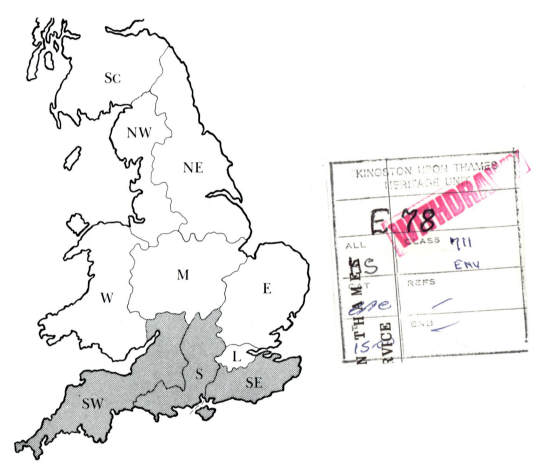

Regions covered in Volume III

Front Cover: Royal Naval Academy, HM Naval Base,
            Portsmouth, Hampshire

Back Cover: Statue of the Duke of Wellington, Aldershot,
            Hampshire

Printed in England by
Saunders and Williams (Printers) Ltd
Hereford House, Beddington, Surrey

CONTENTS

FOREWORD

I welcome the publication of this concluding volume of the PSA Historic Register. Together with the two previous volumes covering the rest of England and Wales, and the companion volume for Scotland, it forms an invaluable record of the historic buildings in use by the Government.

The wealth and variety of the historic buildings included in this volume reflect the strategic importance of Southern England throughout history. The Army and the Navy have both been prolific builders and have also acquired many existing older buildings. It is particularly fortunate that so much remains of our historic naval buildings, some of which were in the forefront of technical development.

Publication of this register illustrates the Government's concern for the conservation of the historic buildings which it occupies and helps to ensure that they will be treated with due consideration.

PATRICK JENKIN
Secretary of State for
the Environment

INTRODUCTION

This is the last in the series of three volumes recording the historic buildings in England and Wales which are occupied by the Crown and are the responsibility of the Property Services Agency; a fourth volume covering Scotland has been published separately by the Scottish Civic Trust.

PSA is responsible for more historic buildings than any other secular body in the country. A relatively high proportion of these are of exceptional interest, being scheduled as Ancient Monuments or listed Grade I or II*. Southern England is particularly rich in government historic buildings including the military concentrations around Aldershot/Camberley and on Salisbury Plain and the major historic Royal Dockyards and their associated facilities and defences. Many of these buildings are still in their original use while others have changed use, possibly several times, and numerous historic buildings which were originally private have come into Crown hands because they or their grounds happened to provide valuable space conveniently located.

Most buildings occupied by civil departments and the Ministry of Defence are in the care of PSA although some clients retain the management responsibility with PSA carrying out work when requested. Government buildings for which PSA has no significant responsibility are omitted from this record; for example buildings owned and occupied by the Home Office, the Health Service and TAVR, those in the guardianship of the Secretary of State for the Environment and the private property of the Royal Family are excluded. Buildings leased by PSA for which the lessors retain the whole maintenance responsibility are also omitted. The Government estate is not static and there will undoubtedly have been changes since going to press.

A broad definition of an 'historic building' has been used to decide which structures to include. Scheduled Ancient Monuments have been included unless they are field monuments of primarily archaeological interest. Listed Buildings of Special Architectural and Historic Interest are included even when they are railings, lamp-posts, statues, ordnance or other features rather than buildings. Buildings have been included which could qualify for listing by current criteria on re-survey. Some traditional and recent buildings have been included for their particular interest even though they may not be of listable quality.

Regrettably many of the buildings in this record are not publicly accessible beyond the demands of the function. Ministry of Defence establishments in particular are almost invariably closed, except in some cases on certain well published occasions, and even then not all areas may be accessible.

The division of this record into volumes generally follows lines where county and PSA Works Region boundaries coincide and where they do not county boundaries have been given precedence. An exception was made for the royal buildings at Windsor which were associated with the London royal parks and palaces in Volume II.

Arrangement of this Volume

This volume is arranged alphabetically by counties. The county and PSA Works Region are given on each page. Entries within each county are arranged alphabetically by town or village and within each of these in alphabetical order of street address.

Entries are headed with the building or establishment name and address, followed by the occupying department and form of tenure. PSA has the full maintenance responsiblity for buildings shown as leased but is only responsible for internal maintenance of those shown as hired, none of which are illustrated.

It is recorded whether an item is a scheduled Ancient Monument and/or a Listed Building of Special Architectural and Historic Interest. The grades of Listed Buildings are given, including the obsolete Grade III and Crown List status where these have not yet been regraded, and whether they have been assessed as having Group Value. It is indicated where a building lies within a Conservation Area, National Park, Area of Outstanding Natural Beauty or Site of Special Scientific Interest.

The material is drawn from a record of historic buildings prepared for maintenance management purposes within PSA by its Conservation Unit. The extent of the descriptions relates the architectural and historic significance and the degree of PSA responsibility for the buildings and little known ones are relatively more fully described. The descriptions are drawn mainly from personal observation and standard references especially the statutory lists of historic buildings and Sir Nikolaus Pevsner's 'The Buildings of England'. References are given in the entries and there is a key to the commonly occurring references on page 8.

ACKNOWLEDGEMENTS

PSA is grateful to the DOE Directorate of Ancient Monuments and Historic Buildings, occupying departments, local planning authorities, the National Monuments Record and local libraries and archives for their help in the preparation of this volume. The descriptions of the buildings in and around the Aldershot/Camberley area were prepared by Mr Stephen Levrant of F G Frizzell and Partners, Architects. Photographs from sources outside PSA have been provided by Mr Stephen Levrant, The National Monuments Record, and the Department of Clinical Photography, RN Hospital, Haslar.

ABBREVIATIONS USED FOR COMMONLY OCCURRING REFERENCES

AMS	DOE Ancient Monuments Secretariat records
Balfour	Alan: *Portsmouth*; Studio vista, 1970
Coad	Jonathan: *Historic Architecture of HM Naval Base Portsmouth, 1700–1850*; Mariners' Mirror, 1981
Colvin	Howard: *Biographical Dictionary of British Architects 1600–1840*; John Murray, 1978
Girouard	Mark: *Life in the English Country House*; Yale UP, 1978
Hogg	Ian: *Coast Defences of England and Wales 1856–1956;* David and Charles, 1974
King's Works	H M Colvin (ed): *The History of the King's Works*: HMSO
Pevsner	Sir Nikolaus, et al: *The Buildings of England*; Penguin Books
RCHM	Royal Commission on Historic Monuments
Sutcliffe	Sheila: *Martello Towers*; David and Charles, 1970
UCHB	Statutory Lists of buildings of special architectural or historic interest prepared by DOE Urban Conservation and Historic Buildings Division
Williams	G H: *The Western Defences of Portsmouth Harbour 1400–1800*; Portsmouth Papers, 1979

LIST OF LOCATION PLANS

BUILDINGS OF EXCEPTIONAL INTEREST IN VOLUME III

ANCIENT MONUMENTS

Bold type indicates groups

Infirmary Stables, Arborfield, Berkshire
Scraesdon Fort, Anthony,
Tregantle Fort, Anthony,
Tudor House, Dartmouth
Rougemont Castle, Exeter
Agaton Fort, Plymouth
Camber and Magazines, Bull Point, Plymouth
Eastern Kings Battery, Plymouth
Crown Hill Fort, Plymouth
Royal William Victualling Yard, Plymouth
Ernesettle Battery, Plymouth
South Yard, HM Naval Base, Plymouth
Morice Yard, HM Naval Base, Plymouth
The Quadrangle, HM Naval Base, Plymouth
Royal Citadel, Plymouth
Mount Batten Tower, Plymouth
Breakwater Fort, Plymouth
Fort Staddon, Plymouth
Fort Bovisand, Wembury
Watch House Battery, Wembury
Master Gunner's House, Portland Castle
Martello Tower No 66, Eastbourne
Ruins of Ore Manor, Hastings
Fort Blockhouse, Gosport
No 5 Battery, Stokes Bay Lines, Gosport
Gunboat Yard, Gosport
Fort Monkton, Gosport
Fort Gilkicker, Gosport
Fort Grange, Gosport
Fort Rowner, Gosport
Fort Elson, Gosport
Priddy's Hard, Gosport
Royal Clarence Victualling Yard, Gosport
King James Gate, Portsmouth
Eastney Batteries, Portsmouth
HM Naval Base, Portsmouth
Fort Southwick, Portsmouth
HMS Vernon, Portsmouth
Spithead Forts, Portsmouth
Brompton Lines, Chatham
Brompton Barracks, Chatham
Fort Burgoyne, Dover
Fort Halstead, Kent
Martello Towers Nos 14, 15, Hythe
Dymchurch Redoubt, Kent
Martello Towers Nos 6, 7, and 9, Shorncliffe
Dovecote, Netheravon, Wiltshire

GRADE I

Old Bank of England, Bristol
Old Council House, Bristol
Creslow Manor, Buckinghamshire
    Chapel at Creslow Manor
Bramshill House, Hampshire
    Gateway, Outbuildings, High Bridge and Gate-
    house at Bramshill House
4 The Close, Winchester
Osborne House, East Cowes
Wakehurst Place, Ardingly
Wiston House, West Sussex
Homefield House, Trowbridge

GRADE II*

Not all the area has been resurveyed since the introduction of this classification.

Custom House, Bristol
Old College, RMA Sandhurst
Poughley Farmhouse, Welford
Custom House, Falmouth
Crown Court, Exeter
Custom House, Exeter
    Custom House Lodge, Exeter
Trafalgar and Ward Blocks, RN Hospital, Plymouth
Custom House, Plymouth
Custom House, Poole
Main Block, RN Hospital, Gosport
St Agatha's Church, HM Naval Base, Portsmouth
Serle's House, Winchester
County Court, Bridgewater
4 Hammet Street, Taunton
St Cuthbert's Lodge, Wells

BUILDINGS OF PRE-GEORGIAN STYLE IN VOLUME III

MEDIEVAL

Rougemont Castle, Exeter
St Mary's Church, Tyneham
Ruins of Ore Manor, Hastings
Manor Farm, Quedgeley
Constable's Gate, Dover Castle
St Mary in Castro, Dover
St Giles' Church, Imber
Barn at Rudloe Manor, Wiltshire

16TH CENTURY

Chantemarle, Dorset
Tyneham Manor, Dorset
Master Gunner's House, Portland Castle
Telescombe Manor, East Sussex
Repton Manor, Ashford
Wakehurst Place, Ardingly
Wiston House, West Sussex

17TH CENTURY

Tudor House, Dartmouth
Custom House, Exeter
  Custom House Lodge, Exeter
The Terrace, South Yard, Plymouth
Royal Citadel, Plymouth
Manadon House, Plymouth
Mount Batten Tower, Plymouth
Bramshill House, Hampshire
  Gateway and Outbuildings at Bramshill House
King James Gate, Portsmouth
Banqueting House, RMCS, Shrivenham
Shrivenham House, Oxfordshire
Woodhouse Farmhouse, Ilton
Wales Farmhouse, Queen Camel
  Barn and Cottages at Wales Farm
Cottage at Ablington, Wiltshire
Bulford Manor, Wiltshire
Lower Manor Farmhouse, Bulford
Barn at RAF Hullavington, Wiltshire
The Old House, Milston
Rudloe Manor, Wiltshire

EARLY 18TH CENTURY

West Court, Arborfield, Berkshire
The Terrace, Morice Yard, Plymouth
Morice Gate and Yard Wall, Plymouth
No 2 and 8 Stores, Morice Yard, Plymouth
St Andrew's Farmhouse, Lulworth, Dorset
Lutton Farmhouse, Dorset
Fort Blockhouse, Gosport
Main Gate and Dockyard Wall, Portsmouth
Police Offices, HM Naval Base, Portsmouth
1–9 The Parade, HM Naval Base, Portsmouth
Statue of William III, HM Naval Base, Portsmouth
Staff Officers' Mess, HM Naval Base, Portsmouth
Serle's House, Winchester
Former Guard Room, Kitchener Barracks, Chatham
Medway House, HM Naval Base, Chatham
Main Gate, HM Naval Base, Chatham
Dockyard Wall and Tower Houses, Chatham
The Terrace, HM Naval Base, Chatham

AVONMOUTH

20 Gloucester Road
Department of Employment, Part Hired

Mid 19th C three storey terrace with shop units on the ground floor. In brick with ashlar detailing and banding at window sill and head levels. Tiled roof with decorated ridge and fine brick and terracotta chimney stacks. At ground floor level the individual frontages are defined by paired banded columns with foliated capitals, each pair beneath an elaborate cartouche with cornice between. Banded columns to window reveals above with dog-tooth decoration to lintels and cast iron guards.

BATH

Empire Hotel, Grand Parade
MOD (Navy), Leased
Conservation Area

1899–1901 by C E Davis, then city architect. Requisitioned in 1939 by the Admiralty. Five storeys plus attics on a prominent corner site, unfortunately adjacent to the Abbey and Pultney Bridge. Sub-Longleat in style and faced in Bath stone with a red tiled roof.

Cleveland House, Sidney Road
Property Services Agency, Freehold
Grade II, Conservation Area

Built c1820 and sold by the Duke of Cleveland to the Kennet and Avon Canal Company as their head quarters in 1841; purchased by the Crown in 1951. Built over the canal tunnel. Two storey five window Bath stone front, the centre three broken forward slightly. Rusticated arcaded ground floor. Simple cornices to first floor windows except central one, which has a pediment on consoles. Moulded cornice and blocking course. Blind windows in side walls, three storey back elevation. *UCHB.*

Empire Hotel, Bath

Cleveland House, Bath

BRISTOL

Old Magistrates Courts, Bridewell
Lord Chancellor's Department, Leasehold
Grade II

1881. Ashlar, with rusticated ground floor, banding
and an intricately carved frieze. Three storeys in
height and seven bays wide, in a 1:3:3 pattern, with the
centre three being recessed. Sash windows with pilaster surrounds. Monumental projecting entrance with
iron gates and semi-circular pediment topped with a
figure of Justice above. Modillion cornice and parapet
with coping stones. *UCHB.*

Old Bank of England, 12 Broad Street
HM Customs and Excise, Hired
Grade I, Group Value, Conservation Area

1844–47 by C R Cockerell, an ashlar facade in the
'Greek Style'. Three bays wide. At high level, a
pediment over the attic which is lit by three recessed
round-headed windows. In front of these, wrought
iron railings over a full width Doric entablature,
turned at each end to form flanking walls and finished
over brackets. Two fluted half-columns in antis enclose
small windows over deeper openings with stone mullion and transom frames. Flanking walls are rusticated
and rest on projecting porches with cornices supporting cast iron features. Studded panel doors in openings with 'battered' architraves. The interior has been
entirely rebuilt. *UCHB.*

Old Magistrates Court, Bristol

Dorset House, Clifton Down
MOD (Navy), Freehold
Conservation Area

C1830. Originally a pair of semi-detached houses.
Three storeys and an attic with ashlar facade and slate
mansard roof. Rusticated ground floor and banding at
first floor level. Six bays, the ones at either end
breaking forward slightly with pediment on consoles
over first floor windows only. Centre four bays recessed slightly with the second floor supported on tall
Doric columns grouped 1:2:3:2:1 with a balcony
running through at first floor level. *Pevsner.*

Dorset House, Bristol

BRISTOL

Old Council House, Corn Street
Lord Chancellor's Department, Leased
Grade I, Group Value, Conservation Area

1822–27. By Sir Robert Smirke in the Grecian style. In
ashlar, five bays, two storeys and an attic. Monolithic
plinth. Doric pilasters between windows and a central
entrance defined by two storey high fluted Ionic
columns in antis. Floral frieze between ground and
first floors. Simple entablature, dentil cornice and
balustrading hiding the attic windows. Central seated
figure of Justice by E H Baily. To the left an addition of
1828 by T S Pope. Again two storeys in height but only
three bays wide. Deep plinth, sill banding at first floor
level, simple entablature, cornice and blocking course.
Central doorway flanked by single storey Greek Doric
columns in antis. The central first floor window has a
pediment over. *UCHB. Pevsner.*

**Gloucester Row Annex to Bridge House, Clifton
Down**
MOD (Procurement Executive), Freehold
Grade II, Group Value, Conservation Area

Mid to late 19th C terrace. Ashlar fronts to older
houses, No 2 of which differs from the remainder and
is late 18th C in character, probably in the original style
of the terrace. Three storeys plus attic behind dormers.
Two bays per house with sash windows in architraves
under a flat cornice supported on brackets. Rustication
at ground floor level with windows in reveals and
rusticated quoins to mark the individual house divisions. Solid projecting porches with entablature on
half-columns. Panelled doors. Ornamental iron balconies to first floor windows and over porches. Heavy
moulded cornice on enriched brackets with balustraded parapet either side of dormers above. Slate
roofs. *UCHB.*

Old Council House, Bristol

Gloucester Row Avenue, Bristol

Felixstowe, Bristol

BRISTOL

Felixstowe.
Lord Chancellor's Department, Leased
Conservation Area

Late 19th C. Three storeys, basement and attic. A substantial semi-detached house in rubble with Bath stone dressings. Windows grouped 1:2:3, with bay windows to ground floor centre and right, and to first floor right. Window sills on corbel brackets. Cornice on deep brackets with cast iron cresting above between dormer windows. Slated mansard roof with ornate chimney stacks.

Custom House, Queen Square
HM Customs and Excise, Leasehold
Grade II*, Group Value, Conservation Area

1836 by Sir Robert Smirke. In ashlar, two storeys in height and five bays wide. Wide central entrance with cornice over coupled pilasters either side of an inset plain doorway. Royal Arms over. To either side a deep plain plinth terminating in continuous sill banding. Rusticated ground floor with flat headed openings for sash windows with glazing bars. Double banding at first floor level above which are five tall round-headed windows linked with an impost band. Quoins. Over all an entablature, modillion cornice and parapet with coping. *UCHB, Pevsner.*

Custom House, Bristol

The Guildhall, Small Street
Lord Chancellor's Department, Leased
Grade II, Group Value, Conservation Area

Dated 1865–70. By T S Pope and J Bindon in Tudor revival style. In ashlar, two storeys high with ornamental slating to the roofs. The frontage to Small Street has nine multi-light stone-mullioned windows with trefoiled sub-arches. Three high pitched attic gables to the left, the end one being over an angular bay. Projecting porch with square tower over, supporting a slated spire with intricate ventilator grilles. A four-centred arched entrance with an oriel window above. Two four-centred arched entrances to the left and another to the extreme right. At high level parapets with blind tracery, a small turret to the right and tall polygonal chimney stacks grouped in pairs. *UCHB, Pevsner.*

Guildhall, Bristol

KEYNSHAM

Milward House, High Street
Department of Employment, Part Hired
Grade II, Group Value

Late 18th C, a former Friends' Meeting House. Two storeys in ashlar with cornice and parapet. Pantiled roof and later brick chimney stacks. Plinth. Four windows, sashes with glazing bars. To right of centre a panelled door with a fanlight in a semi-circular opening, surrounded by an open pediment on Doric pilasters. Wrought-iron lamp bracket over all. An unusual later window to the right on the ground floor, with two sides projecting to a point. A wing of two windows breaking forward slightly on the extreme right. *UCHB*.

WESTBURY-ON-TRYM

Trym Road Chapel
Department of Employment, Hired

Late 19th C. A former chapel now used as offices and adjoining a terrace of listed cottages. Gabled end in squared random rubble with ashlar coping and dressings to windows and doorway. Tiled roof. Central doorway with pointed arch and squared rubble voussoirs over. Three grouped lancet windows over, the central one being taller than the ones on either side. Dressed stone decoration above.

WESTON SUPER MARE

49 The Boulevard
Department of Transport, Hired

C1900. Two storey semi-detached house in random rubble with ashlar dressings. Sash windows with stone mullions and transoms. Dutch gable with ball finial. Red tiled roof with stone chimney stacks with five clay pots.

115 High Street
Lord Chancellor's Department, Part Hired

C1900. Squared rubble with dressed stone detailing. Three storeys, plinth, quoins, modillion cornice and blocking course. Round-headed sash windows to ground and first floors with segmental headed windows above. All with bracketed sills and keystoned.

ARBORFIELD

Infirmary Stables
MOD (Army), Freehold
Ancient Monument

These stables, built 1911–12, have remained in their
original use ever since. They were originally built to
care for sick horses of the Arborfield Remount Depot.
Their construction and architectural quality are unremarkable, but they do still contain a number of original
features such as horse sling supports, adjustable
draught free ventilation system, mangers and stall
partitions. *AMS*

CROWTHORNE

BROADMOOR SPECIAL HOSPITAL
DHSS, Freehold

1860–1863 by Major General Sir Joshua Jebb. Broadmoor is a unique building type. Its origins stem from
an Act passed in 1860 entitled 'An Act to make better
provision for the custody and care of Criminal Lunatics'. This followed a campaign led by the Earl of
Shaftesbury and other social reformers to have criminal lunatics in a separate building rather than amongst
non-criminal patients in other institutions such as

Broadmoor Special Hospital, Crowthorne

CROWTHORNE   **BROADMOOR SPECIAL HOSPITAL**

Gate House, Broadmoor Hospital

Kentigern, Broadmoor Hospital

Bethelem Hospital ("Bedlam"). Broadmoor opened in May 1863 under the management of the Home Office. In 1949 the ownership of Broadmoor was transferred from the Home Office to the new Ministry of Health, its management being taken over by the Board of Control. Under the Mental Health Act of 1959 Broadmoor came under the direct management of the Minister of Health (now the Secretary of State for Social Services). It was designated as a Special Hospital for patients detained under the 1959 Act who 'require treatment under conditions of special security on account of their dangerous, violent or criminal propensities'.

The military engineer Sir Joshua Jebb, who had designed the 'model' prison at Pentonville twenty years earlier, was commissioned to plan and suypervise the building of Broadmoor Hospital. It is a large complex with separate male and female accommodation, the male side being the larger, consisting of a series of secure ward blocks on high ground overlooking a series of terraces. These south-facing terraces are characteristic of Broadmoor's interesting topography. The wards have small round-arched headed windows and string courses, the windows still having their original iron bars. The low-pitch slate roofs meet cornices corbelled out in brick and with brick dentils. The blocks are separated by "airing courts" for exercise, although much of the original open space has disappeared through the insertion of new buildings in the courtyards. The female side is of a slightly different character, a feature being the wrought-iron lattice work on the lower part of the windows with iron

casements in lieu of sashes and bars giving a less harsh appearance. Although all the buildings are strictly utilitarian and institutional in character, many attractive details remain – ornamental cast iron lamp brackets, a mosaic floor in the female side entrance, original joinery and ironmongery and wrought-iron gates.

The chapel in the centre of the range of buildings dominates the terrace. It has some good joinery and brickwork details with minor polychromatic flourishes but is certainly not ostentatious. The chapel is at first floor level, supported on cast iron columns from the recreation room/theatre below. The main entrance gates, flanked by stumpy towers lead through an arch into the entrance court, surrounded by a covered way. The whole complex is surrounded by a high security wall and features of architectural interest are really not apparent from the outside. One detached house of character, previously occupied by the superintendent and known as 'Kentigern' is outside the secure perimeter.

Major redvelopment of Broadmoor started in 1984 with the construction of a new ward block, Medical Centre, Kitchen and Stores, Administration Offices and Gatehouse. During the course of the next ten years the nature of Broadmoor will alter significantly. However, the old Gatehouse and the Chapel will remain largely unchanged and the architectural character of the buildings should be retained so far as is compatible with the aims of the redevelopment, which are to provide humane and decent conditions for the treatment of patients. *Pevsner.*

READING

COLEY PARK HOUSE
Vacant, Freehold
Grade II

Early 19th C, by D A Alexander, altered c 1840. A rather unprepossessing rendered two storey house with a central attic. Varied and asymmetrical elevations as a result of alterations. Arched porte-cochere and small conservatory on the east front, three storey segmental bay on the south and projection with arched ground floor loggia on the west side. Service ranges to the north.

Fine sash windows, retaining their glazing bars except in the south front bow, with curious raised surrounds and keystones on the east and south fronts. Original tripartite doorway on the east side, with fluted mullions, arcaded fanlight and 18th C sun-god mask over. Balustraded parapet over the cornice. Generally flat roofed with slate roofs to the attic and service wings.

Internally, a stone flagged hall with black corner lozenges. The staircase is c 1840 with arcaded first floor landings. Fine marble chimney-piece in the ground floor bow room. Large formal garden to the west, with walls, terracing and steps. The piers at the end of the west wall are c 1800. *UCHB.*

Coley Park House, Reading

Lodges at Coley Park, Grade II

Early 19th C, by A D Alexander. A matching pair of one and a half storey rendered classical pavilions with hipped slate roofs. Cast iron gates and railings.

Lodge at Coley Park

Balmore House, Newlands Avenue, Caversham
MOD (Army), Freehold
Grade II

A large mid 19thC villa of two storeys, basement and attic. Rectangular main block with rendered and painted walls above a limestone plinth; stone dressings, rusticated quoins, window architraves and first floor level cornice. Moulded timber eaves cornice, hipped slate roof. Angled single storey bay windows in the centres of the longer east and west sides, the latter formerly enclosed within a conservatory. The south side has a cantilevered stone ground floor balcony with cast iron panelled railings and columned canopy; the stairs in the centre have been removed.

Attached to the north side is a small two storey extension with apsidal projections on three sides. The interior is rather plain, with half the ground floor area taken up by the centre and stair halls, separated by a screen of scagliola columns. *UCHB.*

Balmore House, Reading

SANDHURST

ROYAL MILITARY ACADEMY

The Royal Military College was established at High Wycombe in 1799 and moved to Marlow in 1802. The site at Sandhurst had been purchased in 1801 but the buildings were not ready for occupation until 1812. In 1947 the College was amalgamated with the Royal Military Academy which had been established at Tower Place, Woolwich Common and had moved to Woolwich Common in 1806. The buildings are described in chronological order; the Terrace and the Main Gate are in fact in Surrey but are included here for completeness. *UCHB, Pevsner.*

The Terrace

The first new buildings for the College, a line of originally thirteen though now only twelve double houses built for the professors in 1808. Three storeys, yellow stock brick with gauged brick flat arches to sash windows, each with a four window front and three bays of blind windows on the side. Deep eaves to pyramidal slate roofs. Known from their tall proportions as 'tea caddy row', they have acquired a variety of extensions and porches.

The Terrace, RMA Sandhurst

Main Gate

1807–12, by James Wyatt or John Saunders who replaced him as architect for the College, in the most austere neo-classical manner. In the centre is the single storey painted stucco guardroom with a simplified Doric seven bay colonnaded front and end returns, sash windows and hipped slate roof. This is flanked by iron gates and railings with piers surmounted by lanterns, beyond which are small square pavilions with recessed Doric columns and a frieze, cornice and low parapet to their pyramidal roofs. The whole is set back from the line of London Road on which are cast iron lamps on solid bases, with their lanterns missing. Now the Staff College Gates.

Staff College Gates, Sandhurst

SANDHURST   ROYAL MILITARY ACADEMY

Old College, RMA Sandhurst

Old College, Grade II*

1807–12 by John Saunders, an early major neo-classical building like an elongated mansion, of two storeys in painted stucco. The projecting centre is fronted by a hexastyle Doric portico in Portland stone with the Royal Arms in the tympanum. On either side are twelve widely spaced windows, the end three bays breaking forward, linked by short set back single storey colonnades to seven bay blocks and three bay terminal pavilions. The low pitched slate roofs are largely hidden by the high parapet above the powerful cornice. The whole building sits on a high basement which is masked by the area wall parapet, on each external angle of which around the various elements are plinths with open-work iron lamp holders.

The main interior spaces are the large plain entrance hall with a vaulted top-lit room over and the former chapel axially behind which is now the Indian Army Museum.

Lampholders, RMA Sandhurst

1–8 Chapel Square

1810, two groups of houses facing each other across the square; each consists of a detached four window fronted house linked by a screen wall to a range of three houses eleven windows wide. Two storeys in yellow stock brick with gauged brick flat arches to sash windows, cornice and parapet.

Lamp Holders, Main Avenue, Grade II

Outliers on the axis of Old College; two baluster-shaped iron lampholders on stone plinths with cannon bollards at the corners.

SANDHURST **ROYAL MILITARY ACADEMY**

Library

The main section was built as a gymnasium in 1862. A tall single storey painted stucco block on a Latin cross plan. The external walls are articulated by plain pilasters with a subsidiary order flanking the high level windows. The gables of the main roof are pedimented. The roof crossing is surmounted by a tall octagonal timber lantern with a copper dome.

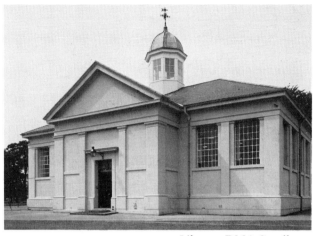

Library, RMA Sandhurst

Royal Memorial Chapel

A most curious edifice. A new chapel designed by Capt Henry Cole to replace that in the main block was dedicated in 1879, of Italianate romanesque style with polychrome brickwork externally and alabaster and marble adornment internally.

Plans to enlarge the chapel were revived after the Great War, as a memorial. Under designs of Capt A Martin, the orientation was changed from south east to north east and the original building became the transept, between balancing additions for sanctuary and chancel and nave porch attached to its flanks, with vestries added behind the original sanctuary. Work progressed as money was donated from 1918 to 1937, the new east end being dedicated in 1921; the proposed tower never materialised.

The extensions are brick externally with limited stone dressings, in a style blending late classical and romanesque elements. The interior is rather spartan and renaissance in detail, the visual interest being largely contributed by the fittings which are all memorials. The redecoration of the original sanctuary after the South African war survives; the organ case of 1950 opposite over the original entrance is by Sir Hugh Casson. The pulpit of c 1900 was retained but repositioned during the enlargement. The mosaic in the semi-dome of the eastern apsidole is by Boris Anrup; there is much interesting modern stained glass.

Royal Memorial Chapel, RMA Sandhurst

SANDHURST   ROYAL MILITARY ACADEMY

New College, RMA Sandhurst

New College

1908–12, an imposing Edwardian baroque group laid out on a gentle curve to the north east of the Old College. Mainly three storeys, the ground floor channelled ashlar with arched openings, the upper parts red brick with limestone dressings. The central block is more elaborate with double height first floor rooms. The centre is pedimented on coupled Ionic columns with the Royal Arms in the tympanum and has a semi-domed porch. Above rises a substantial clock tower with a copper domed octagonal upper stage.

Statue of the Prince Imperial, Grade II

Originally erected at RMA Woolwich in 1888 as a memorial to the son of Napoleon III killed in the Zulu war, moved to Sandhurst in 1947. A uniformed standing bronze figure on a high polished Shap granite plinth with diagonal angle buttresses carrying four bronze eagles. Count Gleichen was the sculptor.

Prince Imperial, RMA Sandhurst

SANDHURST   **ROYAL MILITARY ACADEMY**

Statue of Queen Victoria, Grade II

At the end of Main Avenue. Originally erected at
RMA Woolwich as a memorial in 1904 and removed to Sandhurst in 1947. A standing bronze
figure in state robes on a polished Shap granite
plinth with four bronze reliefs of battle scenes,
around the base. The scupltor was Henry Price.

Kurnool Mortar, Grade II

A huge antique bronze 27″ field piece, excavated at
Kurnool, India in 1839 and moved to Sandhurst
from Woolwich in 1946.

Much of the visual attraction of the Academy lies
in its landscaping which now in its maturity displays
the foresight of those responsible. A Mr
Bracebridge directed the planting and lakes were
formed by damming streams. Fortunately the great
increase in buildings this century has not destroyed
the overall spacious effect.

Queen Victoria, RMA Sandhurst

SHINFIELD

The Lodge, Shinfield Park
Meteorological Office, Freehold
Grade II

1814. Architect unknown at present; built for the
Rev. George Hulme, a chaplain and one-time private secretary to the King of Hanover. The Lodge
went through a number of owners until in 1939 it
became part of Leighton Park School, and then was
requisitioned by the RAF. It remained with the
Ministry of Defence until the Meteorological Office
College was opened in 1970.

The main part of the house is almost square in
plan and not particularly distinguished in its elevations. The interior is very plain with only one large
room with an adjoining conservatory of near contemporary date. There are few original features remaining, and the whole has been abominably
treated in terms of decoration and additions. The
grounds, which once covered 158 acres and contained a series of lakes and woodlands, are now
covered with college buildings, and some remaining
war-time 'temporary' buildings. *UCHB.*

The Lodge, Shinfield Park

SLOUGH

DITTON PARK, Ditton Park Road
MOD (Procurement Executive), Freehold
Crown List

The manor of Ditton is first mentioned in Domesday Book. In 1331 Sir John de Molyns was licenced by Edward III to crenellate, ie fortify, his house and in 1335 to enclose the park. In 1472 the manor reverted to the Crown; at one time it was occupied by Cardinal Wolsey and Princess, later Queen, Mary spent much of her time there between 1517 and 1521.

In 1615 Ditton Park was granted to Sir Ralph Winwood, Principal Secretary of State, who began to rebuild the house in 1617 and greatly enlarged the area enclosed by the moat. The estate passed by the female line to the Dukes of Montague and John, second Duke, enlarged the house.

The mansion was devastated by fire in 1812 and rebuilt in 1813–17 by William Atkinson, a pupil of James Wyatt. The considerable irregularities of the present building suggest that the destruction was not total and the tower on the south side is reputedly a survival of the de Molyns house. The house is mainly two or three storeys, of rendered brick with slate and lead roofs. It is built around three sides of a courtyard which is closed on the north side by a surviving wing of the 18th C house.

It is an early example of 'castellated' gothic style, turretted and embattled and with feeble buttresses. Only the front door and flanking windows are more than superficially gothic, the other windows have Georgian proportions despite their label mouldings and gothic section glazing bars. The three storey octagonal bay on the garden front even has a first floor balcony though with a 'gothic' cast iron balustrade. There are coats of arms modelled in Roman cement dotted around the entrance front.

The chief internal feature is the ground floor gallery behind the principal rooms on the garden front, with wall-shafts and plaster vaulted ceiling; a panel of 14th C floor tiles found nearby is set over the fireplace. The entrance hall was a fine composition with heavily beamed ceiling and secondary doors splayed across the angles; it is now marred by a dividing partition. The main staircase rises the whole height of the house with niched walls and a fine cast iron gothic balustrade.

Stables and Office Blocks

Flanking the entrance court; 18th C, superficially gothicised in the 19C with four-centred arches with towers over, the south are capped with an attractive clock turret. Both blocks are much marred by modernisation.

Admiralty Compass Observatory, Ditton Park, Slough

Gatehouse and Bridge

The 18th C brick bridge leads across the moat to the gatehouse which was gothicised and rendered in the 19th C. It has unfortunately lost the plaster vaulting in the archway.

Garden Buildings

18th C brick walls survive rather mutilated to the east and south of the house. There is an 18th C rusticated brick arcaded summer house at the south end of the former kitchen garden walls and a brick gothic arcaded summer house at the east end of the walk in front of the main south garden front of the house.

Stables at Ditton Park

Chapel

East of the house, beyond the moat. Dated 1817 when it was virtually rebuilt apparently on the site of a medieval chapel. A strange little building, of brick with stone dressings and slate roofed. Undifferentiated rectangular plan with gabled ends and buttressed flanks. The gable ends have massive finials to the angle buttresses, traceried blind windows flanking the central window and empty niches over. There is an empty bellcote at the west end. Now a store.

Ditton Park Road Lodge

A small early 19th C gothic brick building with a tiled roof, on the eastern edge of the site at the end of a fine curving avenue of limes, now rather beyond their prime.

Survivals of minor interest are the remains of the 18th C Pump House and Boat House on the northern edge of the island. Near the south west corner of the island is an apsidal rustic garden shelter, now very decayed. On the south boundary of the site is the ruined base of an 18th C brick Ice House.

In 1917 the Estate was purchased by the Admiralty for the Compass Department which removed from Deptford. The gallery doubles as a museum but the entrance hall has suffered from subdivision. A single storey shack has sprung up in the inner court-yard. The workshops on the north side are unfortunately visible from the entrance court and those behind the stables are prominent from

Chapel at Ditton Park

the bridge. The recent laboratories to the west of the house are more discreet. The approach is marred by car parks, shacks of various function and the Naval Stores compound which are being tackled by screen planting.

SUNNINGDALE

Sunningdale Park
Civil Service College, Freehold

Civil Service College, Sunningdale Park

The history of this house is obscure. It is known that a house was first built on this site in 1830 by a Mr Stewart, and in 1883 a Mr Mackenzie altered and enlarged it. In 1930 the estate was purchased by Sir Hugo Cunliffe-Owen, Bart. (President of British-American Tobacco Co. and Chairman of Cunliffe-Owen Aircraft Ltd) who demolished the former house and built the present one on the old foundations. The Architect was W E Lord.

Although the exterior presents a rather staid version of inter-war Palladianism, and is not particularly distinguished, the interiors are a tour de force of historical eclectisism, running the whole gamut of styles from medieval to 20th century. The effect is one of stunning opulence of a kind which must have been rare even at that time. The centrepiece is the hall, rising through the building and top lit by gothic ribbed vaulting. The joinery is extremely fine thoughout, particularly in doors and doorcases, and

there is a collection of chimney pieces of superb quality and of varying ages and origins. There are also good examples of surviving ironmongery and lighting fittings.

The estate has well landscaped grounds with numerous outbuildings that date from the previous house. The stables are sited where the first house was built prior to 1830. The two lodges, Bothy Cottage, game larder, and charming summer house are all late Victorian. Bothy Cottage and the adjacent game larder are in a very dilapidated condition, the remainder are reasonable.

Sir Hugo Cunliffe-Owen did not live long to enjoy the house as he died in 1947, when it was sold to the Crown. The Civil Service College now uses the building, and fortunately their main campus development is sited some distance from the house leaving it with a most pleasing aspect. *Pevsner.*

CRESLOW

Creslow Manor

CRESLOW MANOR
Diplomatic Service, Freehold
Grade I

The manor house is of great interest and has had a very complicated building history. It is variously of two and three storeys, on a basically T-shaped plan but with projections in all directions. The walls are of poor quality local limestone, with steeply pitched tiled roofs, some plastered dormers and brick chimney stacks.

The site was occupied before the Conquest. The oldest work extant is c 1330, comprising the solar block at the head of the 'T' with its annexes and part of the hall range which forms the stem. The building has been much altered over the centuries, especially in the 16th and 17th C, and even since RCHM. A few minor original windows survive; the heads of several windows are reused 16th C fire place lintels.

The interior has been equally altered. The most notable feature is the 14th C crypt under the east end of the solar block which is tierceron rib vaulted with foliage bosses. The top storey of the house was used as a long gallery; the main staircase is 17th C. *UCHB, RCHM, Pevsner.*

Chapel and Cottage at Creslow Manor

Chapel at Creslow Manor, Grade I

A small rectangular stone block with a tiled roof, near to the Manor. 13th-14thC but as much altered as the house. Some blocked medieval windows remain and are part of a re-used 12th C doorway with zig-zag and billet mouldings.

Walls and Outbuildings, Grade II

The front of the manor has a walled garden and 17th C stone, gate piers with ball finials. There are some small out buildings of stone and timber framed with tiled roofs, part of which is converted to an attractive cottage.

HALTON

Halton House
MOD (RAF)
Grade III

Built in 1884 for Baron Alfred Charles de Roth-schild and occupied by the RAF since 1918. This enormous mansion in 17thC French chateau style virtually defies description. Two storeys, basement and attics, faced in the finest ashlar and crowned with a magnificently complex roofscape. The two main fronts on the north and south have canted bays and a high centre piece; they are identical except for the porte-cochère on the entrance front. Superimposed Doric and Ionic orders run all round the building with free standing columns on the main fronts.

The interior is sumptuous in the extreme. The galleried central hall rises through two storeys to a glazed dome, with a tremendous chandelier. The adjacent stair hall is all in white and gold with bronze balustrades. Other rooms are of matching splendour. There has been much redecoration but it would take a sizeable chunk out of the defence budget to furnish the building to match the opulence of its architecture.

The more modestly scaled service wing survives on the east side but the present west wing was built in 1927 on the site of the huge domed winter garden. A fountain adorned with nymphs survives the rigours of service occupation in a pool in the garden. *UCHB, Pevsner.*

Central Hall, Halton House

Halton House

LATIMER

Latimer House
Vacant, MOD Freehold
Grade II, Area of Outstanding National Beauty

Latimer House

Rebuilt by Edward Blore for the Hon Charles Compton Cavendish, later Lord Chesham, after destruction of an earlier house by fire in 1836. The result hardly does justice to the magnificent site being in Blore's usual substantial but uninspiring Tudoresque style. Two storeys and attic, red brick with limestone dressings, Westmorland slate roofs. Hooded mullion and transom windows, octagonal angle buttresses and crenellated parapets and separate shafted chimney stacks. Regularly planned with a grand central staircase surrounded by a plaster vaulted corridor.

The entrance porch carries a date 1863 when alterations were carried out including terracing across the south front with flint and ashlar walls and pierced balustrades. The irregular service area on the north side of the house incorporates an attractive clock tower with an octagonal bell cupola. The stable block, free standing to the north, has an impressive buttressed wall. *UCHB, Pevsner, Colvin.*

Latimer House

MILTON KEYNES

Stables at Bletchley Park
Department of the Environment, Freehold

Bletchley Park has become famous as the centre of code breaking activities during World War II under the code name 'Ultra'. The late Victorian mansion is now a British Telecom engineering school. The stables behind it are an attractive group of one and half storey buildings round a courtyard, brick with tile hanging and tiled roofs. The entrance is through a timber framed archway with a cross-gabled roof surmounted by an octagonal louvre and weathervane.

Stables at Bletchley Park

ANTONY

Scraesdon Fort
MOD (Army), Freehold
Ancient Monument

Begun in 1859, the northern of the pair of forts defending the neck of the peninsula on the west side of the Hamoaze, which were the only part of the proposed western section of the ring of forts around Plymouth to be built.

The main body of the fort is a regular half-octagon of earth covered casemated ramparts around the upper parade, protected on the vulnerable sides by ditches with caponiers. The middle and lower parades step down the steep slope to the St Germans River on the north side of the fort which is protected from assault from that direction by the river. *AMS, Hogg.*

Scraesdon Fort, Antony

Tregantle Fort
MOD (Army), Freehold
Ancient Monument

Begun in 1858, the southern and larger of the two forts protecting Plymouth from the west. The basic plan is hexagonal with alternate very obtuse and near right angles, symmetrical about its long east-west axis, but cleverly adapted to the requirements of the site. The terreplein is divided into two levels along the axis, as are the defences.

Those around the upper, northern part are masonry revetted earth ramparts and ditches intended to resist attack from the land, with Haxo casemates on the ramparts. The north and north west fronts which are most exposed to attack have an elaborate double caponier at their junction.

The lower, southern half of the fort is intended to prevent a landing on Long Sands or bombardment of the dockyard by ships in Whitsand Bay.

The defences are two-tiered masonry casemates and the south face is flanked by demi-bastions, a very late example. The north east and south east faces form the gorge of the fort, protected by caponiers at their extremities. At their junction is the defensible keep which is circular towards the terreplein and isolated by its own ditch. *AMS, Hogg.*

Tregantle Fort, Antony

ANTONY

Old Ferry Office, Jupiter Point
MOD (Navy), Leased

A delightful early 19th C two storey rectangular block with a semi-octagonal end, porch and single storey wing. In banded rubble with the main walls articulated by shallow pilaster strips with imposts and corbelled segmental arcading. Horizontal sliding sash windows. Deep timber eaves with paired brackets corresponding to the pilasters. Hipped delabole slate roof. Used as a sailing centre.

Old Ferry Office, Jupiter Point, Antony

BODMIN

Victoria Barracks
MOD (Army), Freehold

Begun in 1859, the majority of the barracks has now been demolished and the site become an industrial estate.

A small group of buildings at the apex of the site remains in Army occupation. The main building houses the Regimental Museum of the Cornwall Light Infantry.

It is an imposing rectangular block of rubble with granite quoins, three storeys and attic. Seven window front with Granite window lintels and segmental central archway. Massive hipped slate roof with a single dormer on each face, each with its own pyramidal roof. Red brick chimney stacks on the ridge and at each corner.

The approach is between two small single storey blocks of similar construction and the group is enclosed by a high squared rubble wall with granite archway, musketry loops and coping.

Victoria Barracks, Bodmin

BODMIN

Shire Hall, The Square
Lord Chancellor's Department, Part Hired
Grade II

1837 by Bush of Launceston, a splendid monumental granite ashlar block in very belated neo-classical style. Seven window front, the sides of one tall storey the lower part of which is treated as a rusticated podium above the plinth. The three centre bays are broken forward boldly and two storeyed. The ground floor has archways with iron gates, with the cap of the podium forming an impost band. The first floor windows are a shorter version of those at the side, with elegant architrave surrounds and cornices. The centre piece is pedimented, the sides have a moulded cornice and blocking course largely concealing the hipped slate roof. *UCHB*.

CAMBORNE

Josiah Thomas Memorial
Lord Chancellor's Department, Leased

Late 19th C, tall two storey block, symmetrical front with four window centre between projecting end bays. Granite rubble with ashlar quoins and windows. Painted first floor and first floor sill level band courses, with inscription between. Semicircular headed windows with keystones. Modillion eaves cornice continued on bay end gables. Delabole slate roof.

Josiah Thomas Memorial, Camborne

FALMOUTH

Custom House, Arwenack Street
Customs and Excise, Leased
Grade II*, Group Value, Conservation Area

Early 19th C, on a site sloping steeply down to the Town Quay so that the entrance is at first floor level in a single storey elevation. Unsophisticated neo-classical design with a deep hexastyle Greek Doric colonnade on a granite dwarf wall stylobate with iron railings between the columns. Plain architrave and very deep frieze with the Royal Arms, cornice and a diminutive pediment over the central bay. The actual plain front wall extends two bays further to the right with a quite unsuitable barometer mounting against it. The flank wall is obscured by a public convenience.

The two storey rear elevation is rendered with granite quoins, first floor level band course and hicked flat arched keystoned heads to first floor sash windows. Segmental heads to ground floor openings. Slate roof.

The King's Pipe, Grade II

On the Town Quay beside the Custom House. A square red brick chimney stack in four diminishing stages on a rubble stone base. Used to destroy seized contraband tobacco. The furnace is set within a walled enclosure.

FALMOUTH

Custom House, Falmouth

Coastguard Station, Castle Drive
Coastguard, Freehold

Mid-late 19th C, the station in the centre is flanked by two blocks on either side originally built as barracks but now converted into three houses each. All are two storeys, rendered and painted, with coped gables, slate roofs with dormered ventilators and chimney stacks with heavy cappings. The station has a projecting porch. The houses have cast iron colonnades, now enclosed, supporting a deep first floor balcony. The centre windows of each block are large semi-circles.

Coastguard Station, Falmouth

FALMOUTH

County Court, Market Place
Lord Chancellor's Department, Leased
Grade II

Mid 19th C classical style painted stucco building on an island site. Rusticated ground floor with vermiculated quoins, segmental headed windows and dentil cornice. First floor with rusticated quoins, sill level string course segmental headed windows in moulded surrounds and modillion cornice with blocking course. The taller courtroom block has semi-circular headed first floor windows and low rectangular clerestory windows between the massive brackets of the cornice and a hipped slate roof. The main entrance on the curved junction with the Killigrew Street facade is surmounted by the Royal Arms. Tall chimney stacks with dentil cornices. *UCHB.*

County Court, Falmouth

FOWEY

2 Custom House Hill
Customs and Excise, Leased
Grade II, Group Value, Conservation Area.

A simple small building, mainly 18th C, but having some earlier stonework, attached to the Post Office. Plain granite steps leading up to the main first floor, which has one large corner window and one 19th C double-hung sash. Oval window on river side and stables under with small yard accessible from the river. Slate roof with brick chimneys.

Custom House, Fowey

HELSTON

Leslie House, 9 Lady Street
Department of Health, Part Hired
Grade II, Conservation Area

Mid 18th C granite ashlar house, two storey five window front. Flat arched sash windows and doorway with keystones, first floor level band course. Panelled door with fanlight and side lights. Asbestos slate roof. The famous Hobb House floral dance starts from the yard at the rear. *UCHB.*

HELSTON

Star House, Coinagehall Street
Manpower Services Commission, Leased
Grade II, Conservation Area

C1800 three storey building. The ground floor is
wholly taken up by an acceptable modern double
shop front of granite with aluminium framed glazing. The upper storeys are rendered and painted
and framed by a curious cross between giant pilasters and attached columns, carried on strange fretted corbels and with Ionic capitals and architrave
blocks. The first floor has a pair of splayed cantilev-
er bay windows and the second floor three sash
windows with ornamental apron panels and architrave surrounds. Decorated frieze below a plain timber eaves to the slate roof. *UCHB.*

Star House, Helston

HUGH TOWN, ISLES OF SCILLY

Strand House, The Strand
Customs and Excise, Leased
Grade III

Early 19th C two storey three window stuccoed
house. Stone stairway with cast iron balustrade leading up side to doorway at first floor level with columned surround. Slate roof behind parapet and
band course. Block on right with false masonry
jointed ground floor, rusticated quoins and bracketed cornice to hipped slate roof. *UCHB.*

Lookout Tower, Telegraph Road
Coastguard, Freehold
Grade II

Dated 1814, a circular four storey granite ashlar
tower with four sash windows on each floor. Band
course and parapet. There are various modern excrescences on the top of the tower. *UCHB.*

Coastguard Lookout, Hugh Town

LAUNCESTON

Oddfellows Hall, 14 Western Road
Inland Revenue, Hired
Grade II, Group Value, Conservation Area

Dated 1880. A rectangular hall with a showpiece gable end facade set back from the line of simple cottages with which it forms a piquant contrast. Red brick with painted stucco dressings in an unselective mixture of Italianate classical and romanesque detail, the whole effect charmingly inept.

LISKEARD

Guildhall, Fore Street
Lord Chancellor's Department, Part Hired
Grade II, Group Value, Conservation Area

Designed by Henry Rice in 1858 in typical mid 19th C classical style. Two tall storeys, coursed rubble with granite dressings. Vermiculated rusticated ground floor arcading, semi-circular leaded first floor windows. Angles treated as rusticated pilasters on pedestals. Clerestorey windows in frieze of entablature. Hipped slate roof. A square clock tower rises from the Pike Street elevation in three increasingly ornamental stages, culminating in a massively bracketed cornice broken up over the clock faces and crowned with a pyramidal lead roof. *UCHB*.

14 Pike Street
Manpower Services Commission, Freehold
Conservation Area

A 19th C two storey house. The ground floor is completely taken up by a modern recessed shop front. Rendered and painted first floor with two sash windows with architrave surrounds and bracketed sills. Delabole slate roof.

NEWLYN

Bridge House, Newlyn

Bridge House, Tolcarne
Ministry of Agriculture, Freehold

Two storeys, rubble walling with granite blocks quoins, jambs and lintels. Three regularly spaced four pane sashes on the first floor, the ground floor is less regular with a tripartite sash and wide doorway flanked by simple sash windows. Half hipped slate roof, rather marred by ribbon pointing.

PENZANCE

Trevaar, Alverton Road
Government Offices, Freehold
Grade II, Conservation Area

Early-mid 19th C, a tall square three storey house with a three window painted stucco front above a granite plinth. The ground floor angles are treated as pedestals to the panelled pilasters rising through the first and second floors. Ground floor sash windows with granite sills and plain surrounds; first and second floor sill level string courses and architrave surrounds. Hipped slate roof. Exposed granite rubble walling with ashlar dressings on the rear elevations. *UCHB.*

Custom House, The Quay
Customs and Excise, Freehold
Grade II, Group Value, Conservation Area

Early 19th C, two storey blocks, stepping down the steeply sloping site so the entrance is at first floor level of the front block. Granite rubble with ashlar dressings. The single storey street front has a simple doorway with block pilasters and entablature flanked by sash windows. The lower rear block is painted, with utilitarian casement windows and loading doors to both floors. Both blocks have hipped slate roofs.

Trevaar, Penzance

Custom House, Penzance

REDRUTH

Trecarel, Drump Road
Inland Revenue, Freehold

Late 19th C two storey and attic house. Coursed granite rubble with ashlar quoins and window dressings. Symmetrical three bay elevation with wide end bays broken forward and with splayed two storey bay windows. Gabled slate roof with elaborately fretted barge boards.

The Elms, Green Lane
Government Offices, Freehold

Dated 1900 on gate post. A substantial two storey former mansion of irregular plan and eclectic style in carefully squared granite rubble with ashlar dressings. Varied window forms with ornamental pediments and an equal variety of eaves treatment. Slate roofs, pale yellow brick chimney stacks.

Trecarel, Redruth

The Elms, Redruth

ST IVES

Barbara Hepworth Museum, St Ives

Barbara Hepworth Museum
Tate Gallery, Freehold

Two storey granite cottage on a corner site with a splayed angle. The front of the first floor is set back and rough cast and painted with tall dormered studio windows breaking through the eaves line. Gabled slate roof.

TEMPLE

Abbey Cottage
MOD (Navy), Leased
Area of Outstanding Natural Beauty

A small traditional slate roofed granite cottage up on Bodmin Moor. Two storeys, two rooms each. Marred by a corrugated iron porch.

Abbey Cottage, Temple

TORPOINT

Trevol House, HMS Raleigh
MOD (Navy) Freehold

A most attractive house in its own grounds. The main part is an early 19th C two storey L-shaped block, with a projecting section with splayed angles at the corner. Rendered and painted, with a first floor level band course. Sash windows with glazing bars, with recessed apron panels below those on the first floor. Neo-classical style door surround with recessed panel pilasters. Round headed doorway with fanlight and panelled door. Slate roof with box eaves.

At the rear are two attached earlier two storey wings of painted rubble, forming a U-shaped plan with the main block. The fenestration has been much altered. Further back is a detached range of partly painted rubble buildings, formerly the coach house and stables.

Trevol House, Torpoint

Maryfield Cottage, Coombe Park, Wilcove
MOD (Navy), Leased
Area of Outstanding Natural Beauty

A late 19th C house, two storeys and attic, rough cast and painted, with polychrome brick dressings to the windows, the main ones with hood mouldings. Added timber porch. Delabole slate roof with gabled attic windows, one cable shaped and curved with the bow below.

Maryfield Cottage, Torpoint

TRURO

9-10 Strangways Terrace, Truro

Eagle House, 74–75 Lemon Street
Government offices, Part Hired
Grade II, Conservation Area

A 1963 reconstruction of two late 18th C buildings. Ashlar facade with rusticated quoins, first floor band course and parapet cornice. The fenestration was 'regularised' in reconstruction, depriving the elevation of much of its interest and producing some strangely proportioned windows. The flat elliptical archway in the right hand bay was retained but the doorway was relocated and 'Georgianised'. *UCHB*.

9–10 Strangways Terrace
Ministry of Agriculture, Freehold
Grade II, Conservation Area

One of a series of five pairs of early 19th C painted stucco villas. Four window front to the pair, three storeys and semi-basement, with channelled basement and ground floor, first floor sill level band course, eaves fascia and cornice (missing from No 9) and blocking course. The pairs are linked by set-back coupled porches. Iron railings to area and front steps.

Trevint, Strangways Villas
Lord Chancellor's Department, Freehold

A large late 19th C villa of two storeys and attic. Squared rubble with ashlar quoins. Brick window dressings and bay windows, columniated doorway. Delabole slate roof with decorative bargeboards. Interesting rather than attractive.

ASHBURTON

Penrhyn House, 81 East Street
Department of Employment, Freehold
Grade II, Group Value, Conservation Area

Early to mid 19th C. Two linked buildings, the
main part being the end unit of a terrace of three
storey stucco-fronted houses, with rusticated quoins
and door surround. Thin timber doorcase and
moulded surrounds to the first and second floor
sash windows. Timber modillion cornice to slate
roof. To the left, a plain two storey stuccoed front.
Modern bowed shop windows in both parts. *UCHB*.

Penrhyn House, Ashburton

BARNSTAPLE

19a Alexandra Road
Government Local Offices, Freehold

C1900 and part of a terrace of similar properties.
Two storeys in red facing brick and six bays wide
with sash windows with segmental heads. Ashlar
sills, keystones and banding at first floor and again
at eaves level. Fourth bay in from the left at ground
floor level is round-headed with brick and ashlar
voussoirs and recessed door. Slate roof with brick
chimney stacks.

27 Castle Street
Ordnance Survey, Part Hired
Conservation Area

Mid to late 19th C. Three storeys, plus basement
and attic, in the gothic style. Yellow-buff brick ashlar banding and window surrounds with additional
emphasis provided by blue-black brickwork. Parapet. Slate roof with coped gable ends.

**Army Careers Information Office, 2 Litchdon
Street**
MOD (Army), Freehold

Mid 19th C. A simple yet pleasing two storey building with a painted rendered facade under a slate
roof. Multi-pane sash windows to first floor only,
the ground floor window having been replaced by
one in a modern frame.

2 Litchdon Street, Barnstable

BOVEY TRACEY

76 Fore Street
Department of Employment, Freehold

A late 19th C two storey house in 'vicarage gothic' style. Light red brickwork on a granite plinth with blue semi-engineering brick bands. Dressed sandstone surrounds, mullions and transoms to lancet windows grouped in twos and threes. Bay window to right hand front adjacent to decorative timber entrance porch. Brick relieving arch over ground floor window to left. Red clay tiled roofs to main building, bay and porch. Retaining wall to front garden of rough squared stone with brick and granite capping. 'Gothic' decorative railings.

76 Fore Street, Bovey Tracey

BRIXHAM

12 Berry Head Road
Coastguard, Freehold

Late 19th C. Two storeys in squared rubble with ashlar quoins and surrounds to door and window openings. Sash windows. Pitched slate roof with coped gable ends. Chimney stacks.

12 Berry Head Road, Brixham

5 Fore Street
Manpower Services Commission, Freehold

Late 19th C. Two storeys in brick with ashlar detailing. Three bays with rounded openings defined by rusticated pilasters springing from a rubble plinth. First floor cornice and similar treatment to first floor but with the windows having segmental headed openings. Semi-octagonal bay at first floor corner on right with slate turret surmounted by decorative finial over. At ground floor level an oculus with ashlar surround. Again at ground floor level and to the right a single storey bay matching those described as before. Slate roof with brick chimney stacks.

5 Fore Street, Brixham

BRIXHAM

King's Quay
Coastguard, Freehold
Grade II, Conservation Area

Early 19th C. An L-shaped building on a steeply sloping site emphasising the termination of the harbour on the eastern side. Two storeys at the higher level with more below. In rubble with ashlar surrounds to openings and with two splayed bays to the upper floor on the south west side and one on the north west side. Both these elevations are faced with stucco. Hipped slate roof. *UCHB*.

King's Quay, Brixham

King's Quay, Brixham

CHIVENOR

RAF CHIVENOR
MOD (RAF), Freehold

'Fiddlers Green' Public House

The main part is an attractive late 18th C two storey rendered and painted house. The principal elevation is scored with false masonry joints, three windows wide with a round headed central doorway which has apparently lost a doorcase. The rear elevation has a tall central window illuminating the staircase. Roofed, regrettably, with interlocking concrete tiles. To the rear on the left is a lower, earlier wing with a massive chimney stacks. A walled garden encloses both ranges. To the right is a most unsympathetic modern extension.

Fiddlers Green, RAF Chivenor

Cottages adjacent to 'Fiddlers Green'

Two attached two storey cottages of 19th C appearance. Rendered and painted walls with timber casement windows. Gabled roof, asbestos slated, with some gablets over windows. Massive external chimney breasts suggest the incorporation of an earlier structure.

Cottages at RAF Chivenor

Hawks House, RAF Chivenor

Hawks House

L-shaped rendered and painted two storey farm house. Lower 17th C wing with massive 'projecting stepped chimney stacks, plain 18th C block, gabled slate roofs over both parts.

Thrift Shop

Two storey rendered and painted farm house. The 18th C main block retains its sash windows, the lower later extension has been rewindowed. Slate roofs throughout.

Thrift Shop, RAF Chivenor

DARTMOUTH

Royal Naval College, Dartmouth

Britannia Royal Naval College
MOD (Navy), Freehold
Grade II, Area of Outstanding Natural Beauty

1899–1905, by Sir Aston Webb in Edwardian baroque style, built of Portland stone and red brick on a granite plinth. Three storeys with a central block of five bays surmounted by a central clock tower. Above the entrance are giant columns supporting a segmental pediment emblazoned with the Royal Arms. Windows with stone mullions and transoms. Cornice, stone balustrade and slate roof with dormers. The flanking blocks are joined to the central block by an entablature resting on two Tuscan columns and have triangular pediments over the top storey windows. A single storey block to the left and a two storey block to the right, with flanking towers. *UCHB.*

Royal Naval College, Dartmouth

DARTMOUTH

Custom House, 3 Bayard's Cove Quay
Customs and Excise, Leased
Grade II, Group Value, Conservation Area

The right hand wing of the former Custom House (dated 1739) which although sharing the same roof line is slightly stepped back from the main facade and is probably of a later date. Three storeys in colour washed brickwork with a stucco ground floor and a canted splay bay through the first and second floors. To the right, at ground floor level, a sash window with glazing bars. To the left, a wide entrance with double doors with sculptured Royal Arms and a window at each floor above with glazing bars. *UCHB.*

Tudor House, 5 Higher Street
Department of Employment, Freehold
Ancient Monument, Grade II*, Group Value, Conservation Area

Probably early 17th C. A very fine four storey house with gabled timber front and corbelled stone side walls. A ten-light oriel at first floor level and two four-light oriels at second floor level, all with carved posts and brackets. Some of the original leaded glazing remains. The timber framing is moulded and exposed, except in the gable which is slate hung. Overall a slate roof with a brick chimney stack. *UCHB. See Frontispiece.*

Custom House, Dartmouth

EXETER

ROUGEMONT CASTLE, Castle Street
Lord Chancellor's Department, Freehold
Ancient Monument, Conservation Area

PSA is responsible for the buildings within the castle, the gateway, most of the curtain wall and two of the mural towers but not for the south west curtain, the west tower and the section of curtain immediately north east of it.

William I chose the site of the castle after the surrender of the rebel city in 1086. It is a roughly square enclosure formed in the northern corner of the Roman city wall, formerly with an outer bailey.

The original gatehouse tower is of early date, possibly one of the earliest masonry fortifications in the country. Within the high outer arch are two windows with heads of triangular, Saxon type. The archway below was later blocked as at the comparable keep/gatehouses at Richmond and Ludlow and a new gateway formed on the north side, which was replaced by the present entrance when the Crown Court was built.

There is a polygonal tower at the eastern angle junction with the Roman wall and a half-round one in the middle of the north east curtain, both with pilaster buttresses. The wall was taken down and replaced with iron railings behind the Crown Court. *UCHB, King's Works, D Renn : 'Norman Castles'.*

Crown Court, Grade II*

1774. Main facade of dressed stone, two storeys high and nine bays wide. Rusticated ground floor with round-headed openings, the central three being arches with an open portico behind. This central unit breaks forward slightly with a pediment over the three windows at first floor level. All windows sashed with glazing bars. The rear elevation is in red brick with the centre projecting. Later side wings.

The east wing dates from 1905 and is similar in detail to the main block. Four bays wide with the third breaking forward with Venetian windows on the upper floor and a dentil pediment over. Round-headed sashes with glazing bars. Slate roof with cupola, To the west, a modern wing in red sandstone.

Castlekeeper's Cottage

Dated 1892. A delightful two storey cottage, red sandstone with limestone dressings. Mullioned windows in projecting bays with mock arrow loops in the gables. Modern tiled roof.

Crown Court, Exeter Castle

EXETER

Castlekeeper's Cottage, Exeter Castle

Statue of Earl Fortescue, Grade II

In the castle court, a stone standing figure on a granite plinth, by E Bailey Stephens, 1863.

Earl Fortescue, Exeter Castle

Higher Barracks, Howell Road
MOD (Army), Freehold
Grade II

1792 and 1867. In red brick and of two storeys under slate roofs. Sash windows, some arched, with glazing bars. The north range has a hipped slate roof with central cupola with clock and weathervane. To the east and west, identical ranges with first floor cast iron verandahs and round headed openings below to the former stables. The other buildings within the confines of the barracks are more recent and do little to complement the ranges described above. *UCHB.*

East Range, Higher Barracks

North Range, Higher Barracks

Riding School, Higher Barracks

EXETER

Custom House, The Quay
Customs and Excise, Hired
Grade II* Group Value

Dated 1681 on rainwater head. A red brick two storey building the main facade of which is five bays wide, windows with stone dressings. Stone arcading to ground floor now filled in, and late Georgian sash windows inserted here and above at first floor level (the original leaded windows with mullions and transoms remain at the rear of the building). Central pediment with cartouche and feathers and supporters in tympanum. Deep eaves with brackets, hipped slate roof. At the west end of the front is a modern brick projecting addition as well as a recessed two window front. The single storey brick and stone warehouse which adjoins is probably original. Within, a massive 17th C staircase with turned balusters. The plaster ceilings to the stair-well, Long Room and adjoining room have remarkable pendant fruit, flowers and serpents, supported on wooden pegs and lead wires. *UCHB.*

Custom House Lodge, The Quay
Customs and Excise, Hired
Grade II* Group Value

A two storey, two window red brick front adjoining the Custom House at the east end, part of the same structure and probably contemporary. Sash windows, one hipped dormer with casements. Slate roof. *UCHB*

74 Queen Street
Department of Employment, Freehold
Grade II, Group Value, Conservation Area

Mid 19th C. An ashlar building in classical style, two storeys high. Nine sash windows, grouped 1:3:1:3:1, with pedimented heads at first floor level. Rusticated ground floor with arched doorways. Cornice at first floor level and again at parapet level with balustrade. Roof not visible. A similar four bay frontage to Northernhay Gate but with cornices on consoles over the first floor windows. *UCHB.*

74 Queen Street, Exeter

EXETER

Wyvern Barracks, Topsham Road
MOD (Army), Freehold
Grade II

The Institute in the centre of the north-east range dates from 1804. A fine two storey, five window red brick front with pediment over, surmounted by a square weatherboarded clock tower with octagonal cupola. In the tympanum is a large relief of the Royal Arms with draped flags fronted by recumbent lion and unicorn. Brick dentil cornice. Central round headed doorway with rusticated plaster surround. Sash windows with glazing bars. Slate roof. To either side are modern nine window wings in a matching style. Dating from 1959 but also listed grade II are the red brick walls and the wrought iron gates and lanterns which front onto Topsham Road. *UCHB, Pevsner.*

The Institute, Wyvern Barracks

HONITON

Bank House, High Street
Government Offices, Part Hired
Grade II, Group Value, Conservation Area.

Probably 1830–40. A three storey, three window stucco front. Rusticated ground floor with sash windows minus glazing bars. To the left, steps up to a Tuscan doorcase with radial-bar fanlight. Round headed windows with impost banding and continuous cast iron balcony at first floor level. Banding again just below second floor window sills. Cornice and parapet. *UCHB.*

128 High Street
Department of Health and Social Security, Freehold
Grade II, Group Value, Conservation Area

C1810. A three storey, four window brick facade. Plinth, six-panel door with elliptical radial-bar fanlight in a Greek Doric surround with fluted columns. Sash windows with glazing bars, keyed flat heads. Timber eaves cornice. *UCHB.*

128 High Street, Honiton

ILFRACOMBE

1–2 High Street
Manpower Services Commission, Leased
Grade II, Group Value

Early 19th C. A three storey stucco front, three
windows wide – sashes with glazing bars set within
moulded architraves. Cornice and parapet with slate
roof and dormers behind. Modern shop fronts at
ground floor level. *UCHB*.

1-2 High Street, Ilfracombe

KINGSBRIDGE

20 Fore Street
Department of Employment, Part Hired
Grade II Group Value, Conservation Area

18th C but much altered. Three storeys in narrow
coursed stone, including voussoirs to the flat arches
of the flush framed windows, three at each upper-
floor level but all with modern casements. Contemporary shop front and entrance. Timber dentil cornice and hipped slate roof. *UCHB*.

NEWTON ABBOT

24 Courtney Park
Department of Employment, Part Hired
Grade III, Group Value, Conservation Area

Mid 19th C. This district of the town was laid out
soon after the coming of the railway caused the
town to expand in this direction. It consists of wide
roads and open spaces round which detached and
semi-detached stucco houses are informally
arranged. The buildings are mostly Italianate in

style, but a few are more strictly classical or in a
picturesque gothic manner. Traditionally they are
painted in shades of buff. Owing to generous layout and uniformity of colour this part of the town is
unusually attractive for the period.

Nos 19 to 29 are gabled groups of houses with
gothic and 'Swiss' detail. No 24 is, like the others,
two storeys high with attic accommodation under a
slate roof. Quoins, coped gable ends and a single
storey battlemented bay at ground floor level.

OKEHAMPTON

East Okement Farm
MOD (Army), Leased
National Park

Two storey mid 19th C granite rubble walled farm house. Three bay main elevation with recessed central bay, marred by a storm porch. Gabled slate roof with gablets over the windows, all with heavy bargeboards. Granite farm buildings, all now with corrugated iron roofs.

23 Fore Street
Government Offices, Part Hired
Conservation Area

Late 19th C, forming an end of a three unit terrace. Three storeys, squared granite rubble with ashlar quoins, the front elevation rendered and painted above the shop front and with tripartite sashes on the upper floors. Deep timber eaves to hipped slate roof.

PAIGNTON

4 Palace Avenue
Manpower Services Commission, Freehold

Late 19th C and part of a terrace. Three storeys and an attic in buff brick. Modern shop front. One round-headed first floor sash window with a dressed stone arch and to the left a timber canted bay with pediment over. Stone banding and three segmental headed sash windows with cambered stone heads to second floor. Modillion cornice with stone and brick ornament. Dormers in slate mansard roof.

4 Palace Avenue, Paignton

PLYMOUTH

1-4 Albert Road, Devonport

1–4 Albert Road, Devonport
Property Services Agency, Freehold

Mid 19th C, built as a home for destitute families of soldiers, sailors and marines; the wings were opened in 1874. Five bay four storey centre block with projecting three storey wings, all with lower ground floor. Both phases are in a similar classical style, rendered with painted stucco dressings, string courses and modillion cornices. The centre has architrave surrounds to 12 pane sash windows, the wings have elaborate tripartite windows. Rusticated central entrance arch. Hipped slate roofs; iron area railings.

Agaton Fort, Plymouth

Agaton Fort, Budshead Road
Department of Transport, MOD Freehold
Ancient Monument

The westernmost fully fledged fort of the north east line around Plymouth recommended by the 1859 Royal Commission, though Ernesettle battery lies between it and the Tamar. Pentagonal in plan with ramparts and ditches protected by caponiers on the sides towards the once open country to the north and a gorge wall to the rear. Haxo casemates were provided for part of the main armament but the fort was never armed. The terreplein has been levelled and the entrance arch destroyed to permit it to be used as an HGV Testing Station. *AMS, Hogg.*

Agaton Fort, Plymouth

PLYMOUTH

Camber Magazine, Bull Point

Camber and Magazines, Bull Point RNAD
MOD (Navy), Freehold
Ancient Monuments

The late 18th/early 19thC camber dock is a rectangular tidal basin enclosed by two L-shaped granite arms with a central entrance. The contemporary magazine on the quayside is a monumental block of squared limestone rubble with pitched-faced dressings containing two barrel vaulted chambers under a single gabled roof. The internal walls retain their match-board linings.

Down stream between Bull Point and Kinterbury Point is an impressive group of five magazines and their associated blast structures probably dating from the first half of the 19th C.

Eastern Kings Battery, Camber Road, Stonehouse
MOD (Navy), Freehold
Ancient Monument

A battery of 1779 rebuilt on the recommendation of the 1859 Royal Commission in granite ashlar and brick work. The 'keep' at the rear is connected to the battery proper by curtain walls with musketry loops and the whole surrounded by a moat. Made redundant in the 1880s by the rapid increase in the power of artillery.

Eastern Kings Battery, Stonehouse

PLYMOUTH

ROYAL WILLIAM VICTUALLING YARD
Cremyl Street, Stonehouse
MOD (Navy), Freehold

1824–34 by Sir John Rennie. The layout designed
to provide in separate buildings but in one circums-
cribed area all the industries needed for the victualling of the fleet, a considerable advance on anything
that had existed before. Covering in all some 16
acres, of which six were reclaimed from the sea, the
complex was to include a bakery and flour mill, a
brewery, slaughterhouse and a large cooperage. In
all a fine architectural exercise which still retains
much of its original glory, *AMS, UCHB, Pevsner.*

Main Gate, Royal William Yard

Main Gate, Ancient Monument

The main entrance to the yard designed by Sir John
Rennie. Massively monumental in banded granite
and surmounted by a statue of King William IV.
Central archway flanked by low wings again rusti-
cated, and pierced by single flat headed openings.
Decoration in the form of bulls heads.

Slaughterhouse, Ancient Monument

A single storey building on a north west – south
east axis. The south east axis forms the pavilion to
the north colonnade entrance. Nineteen bays, tapering to one bay in width at the north west end.
Plinth, stringcourse, cornice and small parapet with
slate roof behind supported on queen posts. The
clerestory on the top of the roof has had its ventilation louvres replaced by plastic sheeting. The west
front has a series of shallow arcading with semi-
circular heads. Within these heads are semi-circular
windows with early forms of iron glazing bars.
Below are five doorways, the double doors possibly
being original.

Slaughterhouse, Royal William Yard

PLYMOUTH

ROYAL WILLIAM VICTUALLING YARD

Police Buildings, Ancient Monument

Two buildings to the south of the main gate, the colonnade on that side connecting the two. The main building, approached through the colonnade, is of two storeys and has a mansard roof with dormers on each side. Granite. Five bays with the original doors and sash windows. The south west block is slightly lower, but again with mansard roof with dormers.

Police Buildings, Royal William Yard

Bakery and Mill Building, Ancient Monument

One of a pair of rectangular blocks flanking the Basin. On the north west side, facing the estuary, is a projecting wing. Three storeys in granite. Rusticated ground floor with a string course above from which pilasters rise to form round-headed arcading above the top storey. Cornice and parapet, behind which are valley roofs, some with their original slates. Windows, apart from a few in the loft space of the mill are modern steel-framed ones. The adjoining mill building is five storeys high and the central chimney still survives.

Bakery and Mill Building

Bakery and Mill Building, Royal William Yard

PLYMOUTH　　　　　　　　　　　　ROYAL WILLIAM VICTUALLING YARD

Central Basin and Swing Bridge, Royal William Yard

Central Basin, Ancient Monument

The central basin for the Royal William Victualling Yard with walls faced with rusticated granite blocks and the corners are curved. Vertical rubbing strakes. The projecting arms have two flight stairs on their southern sides and the double swing-bridge spans the entrance.

Swingbridge, Ancient Monument

A cast iron swingbridge over the entrance to the Victualling Dock, built by Horseby Iron Co, near Birmingham, and similar in design to the one dated 1838 over the Camber in the South Yard at Devonport. This example is probably part of Rennie's original design for the Victualling Yard. The two halves of the bridge run on small wheels, the motion being provided through a crown pinion mechanism. The bridge is now unused and is permanently open.

Brewery, Ancient Monument

Situated to the west of the Basin and forming the balancing block to the Bakery and Mills building. The original design had an open courtyard approached from the south but this has subsequently been filled in with modern building. The detailing of the building is the same as the Bakery and Mills block, but it is lower by two storeys at the north end. Nineteen bays by fifteen. Mostly modernised windows but the chimney remains intact.

Clarence Landings Steps, Ancient Monument

An apparently little used set of steps in the south west corner of the yard. They form a double curving flight leading down into the water. At their head, a large gateway flanked by pilasters. Round the head of the steps are elegant curved railings with a trident motif. The double iron gates are well maintained and have fouled anchor emblems in their centres.

Bakery and Mill Building and Melville Square

Clarence Store, Ancient Monument

A long three storey building, twenty five bays by four, running north-south along Clarence Wharf. In granite with a plinth, two string courses, rusticated quoins and a heavy projecting cornice. The windows to the ground floor are segmental-headed and those above square headed. The west side of the building faces the Tamar River and has consequently been given a suitably grandiose front. Little alteration internally and external works confined only to the substitution of metal framed windows.

Armament Depot, Ancient Monument

An irregular five-sided range of buildings with a courtyard in the centre. The outer ranges have two storeys and are granite built. In the centre of the courtyard is the old smith's shop with its own small central courtyard. This has now been roofed over and has various later additions to it. The external elevations of the main ranges are largely intact, though the roadway to the east side between this and Melville Square has been infilled by a more modern building. Originally these buildings formed the Cooperage and Blacksmith's area of the Yard.

Clarence Store, Royal William Yard

Melville Square, Royal William Yard

Melville Square, Ancient Monument

The central block and focal point of the Victualling Yard. It is built around a large courtyard, and as well as providing storage space, it also houses most of the Victualling Offices. Three storeys with plinth, two string courses, projecting cornice and small parapet, behind which is a pitched slate roof. Nineteen bays east-west and eighteen north-south. The three central bays on the north front are broken forward and flanked by rusticated pilasters. The central bay has a monumental archway carried up to the second storey above which is a tall clock tower with copper sheathed dome. The two bays flanking the carriageway have square-headed double doors which are probably original. In the courtyard more of the original doors to the loading bays survive.

Coal Vaults, Ancient Monument

These seven structures form part of Sir John Rennie's original design for the yard. They are basically granite-built barrel vaulted structures braced by large buttresses, and in some cases still with early double doors. The entrance arches have Gibbs–type detailing.

Royal William Residences, Ancient Monument

A pair of officers' houses near the main gate. Basement, two storeys and an attic, in Penryn granite with a mansard roof. Square on plan with a west front which is five bays in width. Rusticated ground floor. Sash windows largely intact and dormer lights to attic. Front doors approached by flights of steps. Massive chimney stacks.

Royal William Residences

PLYMOUTH

South East Sea Wall, Royal William Yard
Ancient Monument, Grade II

Sea wall on a gentle curve, built of large random stone blocks. Heavily battered and curved in section. Rising from beach to top string course which is round in section above a low parapet with coping. Admiralty Road runs along the top. Segmental archway through to the Victualling Yard.

Crown Hill Fort, Crown Hill Fort Road
MOD (Navy), Freehold
Ancient Monument

The largest fort occupying the key central salient position in the north east defensive line around Plymouth, built on the recommendation of the 1859 Royal Commission on the defence of the United Kingdom. A large irregular seven sided polygonal trace with immense revetted rampart and ditch flanked by five single and a double caponier. The elaborate neo-Norman entrance archway leads to a ramp up to the terreplein with two storey casemated barracks. *AMS, Hogg.*

Crown Hill Fort, Plymouth

PLYMOUTH

ROYAL MARINE BARRACKS, Durnford Street,
Stonehouse
MOD (Navy), Freehold

Established in 1784 but with mid 19th C additions,
a complex of large blocks built around a parade
square. *UCHB*.

Railings along Durnford Street
Grade II, Group Value

Mid 19th C. Large cast iron railings with arrow-
head shafts. Stanchions with ball finials with crown
surmounted by lion.

Archway Block, Royal Marine Barracks

The Archway Block, Grade II, Group Value

Mid 19th C, in stone with ashlar quoins and dressings. The east elevation which faces the parade
ground is three storeys high with an attic and basement, parapet, cornice and slate mansard roof. Central round entrance arch with narrow flanking foot-
way arches, one either side, with medallions above.
The centre is pedimented with five tall round
headed windows below and the whole feature
breaks forward slightly. At each end of centre is a
projecting clock tower with a tent-shaped roof, one
has a wind dial instead of a clock. At the ends two
storey wings, with an arcaded ground floor, connecting end blocks of three storeys and an attic with
pediment and a projecting three storey porch with
segmental pediment. All sash windows with glazing
bars in plain architraves. Fine area railings. The
Durnford Street elevation is similar but with carved
coat of arms in central pediment and without clock-
towers.

Archway Block, Royal Marine Barracks

East Block, Royal Marine Barracks

North and East Blocks, Officers' Mess,
Dining Hall and Single Officers' Accommodation
Grade II, Group Value

Late 18th C. With the Officers' Residences and the
Archway Block forms a complete square. The East
Block, facing the Archway Block is of three storeys
in height over a basement. Forty five windows, all
sashes with glazing bars, in plain architraves. Built
in stone rubble with rusticated quoins and banding
at first floor level. Parapet with slate roof behind
with hipped and gabled ends. The centre breaks
forward slightly with a wide pediment and rusticated central doorway beneath a cornice on brackets. Slight three-window projections near the ends
of the facade. Including area railings.

To the north side of the square the detached
North Block, again dating from the late 18th C.
Similar in appearance to the East Block but without
a pedimented centre. Twenty nine windows and
plain segmental arched entrances. Including area
railings. At the west end at the rear a four storey
tower with a narrow round arched window in the
top storey and a slate hipped roof.

The Single Officers' Accommodation and Mess is
on the south side of the square and at right angles
to the East Block. This too dates from the late 18th
C. Similar to the North Block but with sixteen windows, no pediment and three rusticated doorways
(one of which has been converted to a window).
Including area railings. A 19th C wooden glazed
porch with pediment connects the Officers' Mess to

the East Block. Attached to the rear on the south
east corner is the Dining Hall, again late 18th C. A
rectangular block part cement rendered and part
rubble with quoins and a parapet. It consists of a
basement with the dining hall above lit by five tall
round headed windows at the sides; three similar
but blind at the ends. The centre of the side windows is in slight projection with a parapet over
ramped up to surmounting chimney stack. Segmental arched windows and doorways to basement. The
interior is panelled to dado level. There is a large
pedimented doorway at the end of the hall and a
coved ceiling which was destroyed in the blitz and
now rebuilt.

Officers' Residences (Seven flats)
Grade II, Group Value

Mid 19th C at the south west corner of the square
and in stone with ashlar dressings and quoins.
Three storeys high, attics and basements. Nine windows wide with the right hand three projecting
slightly with a fourth floor above a cornice. Parapet
and cornice. String course at first floor level. Two
entrances, one of which is blocked, with stone pilasters and entablatures. Glazed segmental archway on
the left with three-light windows above; all sashes
without glazing bars and in plain architraves. Including area railings. This block is attached to the
Officers' Mess so completing the square.

PLYMOUTH   ROYAL MARINE BARRACKS

The Globe Theatre, Grade II

Early 19th C brick building thought to have been built as a bowls court. Converted into a theatre in the mid 19th C when the original building was used as the auditorium and the stage was built to the east. The east elevation is in rubble with a gable ended roof of new interlocking tiles with glazing in the gable ends. A large central round archway with corbels at impost and pedimented treatment above. Large double stage doors (through which the scenery passed) with string course continuing at impost level. At each side of the central door and above the string course is a three-light opening, now blocked, above which is a doorway under the eaves with platform and fire escape ladders. There are two small segmental arched windows at ground floor level.

A small circular auditorium, seating approximately 250, with a shallow domed ceiling supported on cast iron columns with the circle also supported in a similar manner. Fluted pilastered proscenium with panelled sides and mock doors with pediments. The auditorium dome is of timber construction under a hipped roof with cast iron trusses.

Long Room, Royal Marine Barracks

The Long Room, Grade II

Built in the reign of George II as an Assembly Room. Two storeys and a basement. In brick with rubble plinth, stone rusticated quoins and banding at first floor level, parapet and stone cornice. A long building with the main entrance facade at the end. Three windows, sashes with glazing bars in openings with rubbed flat brick arches at first floor level. The ground floor windows have moulded architraves. Steps approaching a central entrance porch above a rusticated round headed basement entrance. The entrance porch has Tuscan columns supporting a pediment with dentilled cornice and pulvinated frieze, semi-circular arched doorway with fanlight. Side elevations of ten windows, slightly projecting at opposite end to entrance front. Slate hipped roof. The interior, of one long room on each floor, has been completely modernised.

Globe Theatre, Royal Marine Barracks

No 8 Officers' Quarters House, Grade II

An early 19th C stuccoed house. Coped gable front with heavy cornice. Three storeys high. Three windows, the right hand window in a projection over the entrance with large round headed fanlight and margin lights to glazed door. Sash windows with glazing bars and segmental arches but round arches to window on right above entrance and to small attic window in gable above cornice. Slate roof, hipped over wing at rear.

No 9 Officers' Quarters House, Grade II

An early 19th C stuccoed house with parapet and heavy cornice. Two storeys in height. Three windows, sashes with glazing bars, stone sills. Central wooden porch with cornice, glazed sides and door.

Globe Theatre, Royal Marine Barracks

PLYMOUTH

ERNESETTLE RNAD, Ernesettle Lane
MOD (Navy), Freehold

Ernesettle Battery, Ancient Monument

Built in 1866 as the westernmost position on the
north east defensive line around Plymouth recommended by the 1859 Royal Commission. An irregular polygon on plan with massive ramparts to the
field, flanked by a caponier, and casemated barracks
in the gorge. *AMS, Hogg.*

Ernesettle House

Early 19th C two storey and attic, rendered and
painted house. Three window front with rusticated
quoins and modillion eaves cornice. Keystones
architraves to sash windows. Porch on gable end
with pilastered doorcase. Steeply pitched slate roof.

Ernesettle House, Plymouth

Gateway, Bull Point Barracks

Bull Point Barracks, Foulston Avenue
MOD (Navy), PSA, Freehold

Built as an artillery barracks. Granite dressed
squared limestone rubble entrance arch flanked by
small pedestrian and blind arches within a
pedimental screen with the date 1857 and monogram VR on the keystone and the arms of the

Board of Ordnance in the tympanum.

The red brick slate roofed magazine is in a small
enclosure set against the west side of the walled
barrack area and flanked by gunshed. Five bay two
storey red brick hipped slate roofed former Officers'
Mess in the north west corner. Two rendered two
storey hipped slate roofed former barrack blocks
within the northern half of the compound.

PLYMOUTH

HM NAVAL BASE, Granby Way, Devonport
MOD (Navy), Freehold

The following extremely brief summary of the history of the Royal Dockyard and description of its historic buildings in no way does justice to their importance and interest. Devonport is the youngest of the three major historic dockyards. Plans made by Sir James Bagge in 1625 for a yard at Saltash came to naught. Charles II's visit in 1677 with the intention of establishing a yard had no results.

In 1688 William III and the Duke of York, then Lord High Admiral, visited the site and work began in 1691 on the construction of a basin and dry dock in a natural inlet on the site of the present No 1 Dock and Basin. Buildings erected between 1693-98 included the Terrace and a now replaced Ropery and Great Square Store.

In 1718 the Board of Ordnance, part of the War Department not the Admiralty, moved the Gun Wharf from Sutton Pool to a site north of the Dockyard purchased from Sir William Morice. The Admiralty did not take over Morice Yard from the Army until 1937 and it was not linked to the rest of the naval base by flyovers across the intervening public roads until 1963–64.

By 1727 a further 19 acres had been added to the south of the initial 35 acres of the dockyard. Between 1761 and 1780 the total area grew to the 70 acres at which what is now the South Yard remained until after the last war. By the end of the 18th C the water front was lined with dry docks and building slips and the interior of the yard massively built up with offices, stores and workshops including the twin ropery complex.

Many of the slips and docks were covered in the early 19th C and piecemeal development continued in the South Yard. However the coming of steam driven ships required development for which there was no room in the existing yard which being hemmed in by the town of Devonport was unable to expand. Forty acres were acquired at Keyham, ½ mile to the north. Work began in 1844 and by 1853 two basins, 3 docks, the Quadrangle and Offices were in operation. A tunnel was built under the intervening town and Morice Yard in 1854–56 to link the two section of the Dockyard.

In 1896 work began on the 114 acre Northern Extension, completed in 1907 with its docks and two basins. The whole yard suffered extensively from bombing during World War II. North and South yards were both extended during rebuilding to take in 40 acres of the town between them.

Despite the heavy wartime losses there are still buildings of great interest in the Naval Base, especially the ropery complex and covered slips, and Morice Yard is an early and the only relatively intact Gun Wharf. Most of the historic buildings have been scheduled as Ancient Monuments, which with the exception of the Quadrangle in North Yard are confined to South Yard and Morice Yard. The three yards are described in their order from south to north with the buildings in each being so far as possible in chronological order. *AMS, UCHB.*

SOUTH YARD

The Terrace, Ancient Monument, Grade II

1692–96, the oldest and once the finest dockyard terrace. It originally consisted of thirteen houses with lower return wings at each end. The Commissioner's House in the centre and the two pairs either end were broken forward boldly, pedimented and pavilion roofed. The front had been rendered and repainted and the windows renewed before all but the northern pair and their return were destroyed in the blitz.

The two surviving houses form an eight bay, three storey and basement front with quoined angles and first and second floor level band courses, modillion eaves cornice and blocking course. The four central bays are broken forward slightly and pedimented, with carved armorials in the tympanum. Rebated sash windows, with segmental heads except on top floor. Enclosed Doric porches in outer bays of centre. The northern house still retains its original massive steeply pitched hipped slate roof. The southern house lost its already altered roof in the war and now has a low pitched slate roof.

The return wing has no quoins or band courses and a plain moulded eaves cornice with a semicircular pediment (the Commissioner's house had a segmental one) on the south side with armorial carving in the tympanum. It retains its original roof form.

Fore Street Gate

The flanking arches of the gate on the site of the original Dockyard entrance survive but the centre has gone.

PLYMOUTH   HM NAVAL BASE SOUTH YARD

The Terrace, South Yard, Plymouth

Dockyard Wall, Ancient Monument

Mid 18th C. A massive rubble masonry wall averaging 20 foot high with a curved coping. It defines the extent of the pre-war South Yard. The northern part of the east side has largely vanished in the post-war expansion but to the east of the Ropery complex it is in good condition. To the east of the south end of the Ropery is a segmental headed brick lined archway, probably a later insertion. The double doors retain their original wooden lock.

Joiners Shop, Ancient Monument

C1766, the only relatively intact survivor of the three Hemp Houses used for storing raw materials and possibly the completed products of the adjacent Roperies. Two storeys above lower ground floor, limestone rubble with ashlar dressings, rusticated quoins, floor level band courses, entablature and coping. Twin gables at south end and vestigial pediment at north. Ashlar surrounds to arched windows and door ways with keystones and impost blocks. Some windows retain their early metal frames but many have been altered or bricked up, as have the doorways. The roof has been renewed since bomb damage.

Dockyard Wall, South Yard, Plymouth

Joiners Shop, South Yard, Plymouth

PLYMOUTH

East Ropery, South Yard, Plymouth

West Ropery, Ancient Monument

C1766, built as the Laying House, 1200 foot long. Bombed in the war so that only the undercroft remains, a series of stone faced brick vaulted cellars accessible from the lower road on the West side of the building. They were used for storage of tar used in ropemaking.

No 24 Store, South Yard, Plymouth

East Ropery, Ancient Monument

C1766, built as the Spinning House, burnt out and rebuilt by Edward Holl, 1814. Originally 1200 foot long, the northern third was demolished after bomb damage. Three storeys, limestone rubble with ashlar dressings, rusticated quoins, cornice and window and door surrounds. The interior is of 'fireproof' construction with stone slab floors supported on an iron frame, possibly the largest to have been built by that date. Some pulleys from the ropemaking process remain in position.

No 24 Store, Ancient Monument

C1766 as the White Yarn Store, the northernmost of a row of four important buildings related to the roperies. Two storeys, limestone rubble with ashlar dressings, rusticated quoins, first floor and parapet level band courses and cornice, segmental headed windows and doorways. Massive gabled king-post roof.

No 25 Store, Ancient Monument

C1766 as the Tarring and Wheel House. Two storeys, limestone rubble with ashlar dressings, rusticated quoins, first floor and parapet level band courses, cornice coping and pedimented gables, segmental headed doorways and windows. Linked to adjacent No 26 Store by a slightly later monumental rusticated archway. The interior is divided by a crosswall and vaulted. The south half contains remains of tread(?)wheel supports. Converted into an execution chamber at an unknown date, the trap and mechanism are still in situ.

No 26 Store, South Yard, Plymouth

No 26 Store, Ancient Monument

C1766 as a Tarred Yarn Store. Two storeys, limestone rubble with ashlar dressings, rusticated quoins, first floor and parapet level band courses, coping, and segmental headed doors and windows. Massive gabled roof. Still surviving in the roof trusses are the large wooden rollers along which the yarn was wound.

No 27 Store, Ancient Monument

C1766 as a Tarred Yarn Store. Very similar to No 26 store but with an ornamental south facade, stepped gable, with ball caps on the ridge and on pinnacles at the edges. The interior still contains its boarded wall linings and rope winding gear in the roof.

No 25, 26, 27 Stores, South Yard, Plymouth

PLYMOUTH   HM NAVAL BASE SOUTH YARD

Turncock's Residence

1772–73, for the Master Ropemaker, sited at the north end of the Ropery complex. Three storeys and attic, limestone rubble with ashlar dressings, rusticated quoins, band courses, coping, window architraves. Hipped roof with dormers.

The Covered Slip, Ancient Monument

The slip of c1763 covered in c1814, the oldest surviving covered building slip in any Royal Dockyard. The roof is supported on a double line of 23 trussed timber columns. The lead roof covering was renewed in 1967.

Covered Slip, South Yard, Plymouth

King's Hill, South Yard, Plymouth

Museum

Early 19th C as the Dockyard Superintendent's Offices. Three storey block, limestone rubble with ashlar dressings, rusticated quoins, first and second floor level band courses, surrounds to segmental headed doorways and windows. Deep timber eaves to hipped slate roof.

King's Hill, Ancient Monument

1822 to commemorate a visit by George III. A small gazebo built on a natural rock left upstanding when the surrounding level was reduced in the 1760–80s, approached by a winding path past a grotto and ornamental fountain. A circular timber Doric collonade encloses a room with four concave sides. One intercolumnation is occupied by a clock face. The concave tent roof is lead covered.

PLYMOUTH   HM NAVAL BASE SOUTH YARD

No 1 Dock, Ancient Monument

Reconstructed in 1834 on the site of the first dry dock at Devonport which was built between 1691 and 1693. The original works were part of a wet and dry dock complex modelled by Edward Drummer, Naval Officer and Surveyor of the Navy, on similar work at Toulon.

Swing Bridge, Ancient Monument

1838, across the Camber which formerly led to the Boat Pond. Cast iron bridge in two sections on massive rusticated masonry piers projecting into the Camber. The outer faces inscribed 'Horseby Ironworks (1838) Near Birmingham'. No longer operative.

The Scrieve Board, Ancient Monument

Building slip c1830, covered c1840. A large timber structure with a later corrugated metal covering, the slip is now floored over.

South Saw Mills, Ancient Monument

C1847. Two storey limestone ashlar block, parapet cornice. Both storeys arcaded, with segmental heads on first floor. Pilaster angle buttresses. Considerably altered.

Main Dock Pump and Pneumatic Store, Ancient Monument

1851, the best preserved of the monumental Victorian pumping stations at Devonport. Limestone ashlar and coursed rubble above a granite plinth. The pumphouse is a squat three storey tower with a massive bracketed main cornice and moulded eaves cornice. The ground and first floor each have two deeply recessed windows on each side with VR on the apron panels. The attic storey has a row of four oculi on each side. The lower wider former boiler house attached to the north side has a cornice and blocking course and pedimented gable with ball finials. The pumping machinery was modernised in 1931 and the boiler house is now a pneumatic store.

Scrieve Board, South Yard, Plymouth

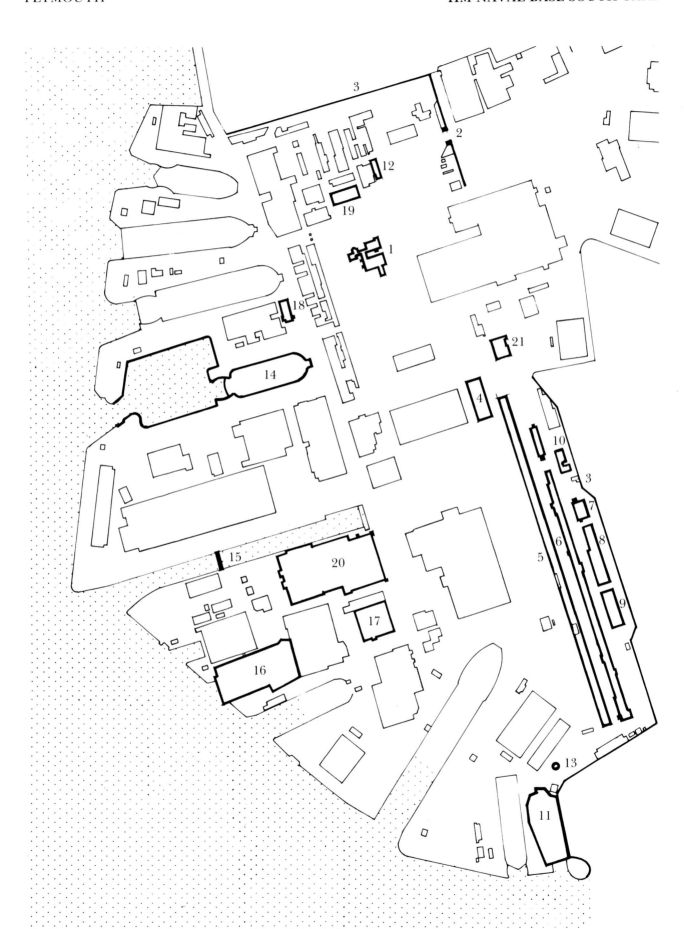

PLYMOUTH   HM NAVAL BASE

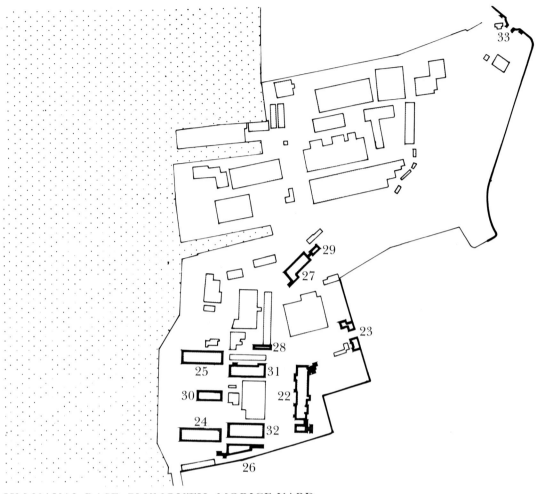

HM NAVAL BASE, PLYMOUTH, MORICE YARD

South Yard

 1 The Terrace
 2 Fore Street Gate
 3 Dockyard Wall
 4 Joiners Shop
 5 West Ropery
 6 East Ropery
 7 No 24 Store
 8 No 25, 26 Store
 9 No 27 Store
10 Turncock's Residence
11 Covered Slip
12 Museum
13 King's Hill
14 No 1 Dock
15 Swing Bridge
16 Scrieve Board
17 South Saw Mills
18 Main Dock Pump and Pneumatic Store
19 Former Fire Station
20 South Smithery
21 Dockyard Lower School

Morice Yard

22 The Terrace
23 Morice Gate
24 No 4 Store
25 No 8 Store
26 No 2 Store
27 No 16 Store
28 No 12 Store
29 No 17 Store
30 No 5 Store
31 No 6 Store
32 No 3 Store
33 North Gate

Old Market Hall, South Yard, Plymouth

Former Fire Station, Ancient Monument

1851. Three parallel blocks, the single storey wings linked by archways to the two storey centre. Limestone rubble with ashlar dressings, rusticated quoins and arches, cornices with blocking courses, pedimented gables, window surrounds, mainly segmental. Slate roofs. Marred by alterations. Now used for storage.

Old Market Hall, Ancient Monument

1852 by Piers St Auybn, on the site of the market hall of 1762; taken into the Dockyard after the last war.

Old Market Hall, South Yard, Plymouth

South Smithery, Ancient Monument

1857. Large cast iron shed with limestone rubble infill to lower parts of side and back walls and piers at rear angles. The two storey front elevation has ashlar dressings, rusticated quoins, window and door architraves.

The Dockyard Lower School, Ancient Monument

C1867 as boiler house for the Roperies. Three storey block, limestone rubble with ashlar dressings, quoins, eaves cornice with blocking course, pedimented gables, window and door surrounds. A second storey projection on one corner is supported on tall Tuscan columns. Badly damaged in the war and never fully restored.

PLYMOUTH

The Terrace, Morice Yard, Plymouth

The Terrace, Ancient Monument

C1720. An unusual row of houses built between 1720 and 1723 to house the senior officers of the Ordnance Yard. The architect is not known. Like all other early buildings in the Dockyard, the terrace is built of locally quarried dunstone.

Morice Gate, adjoining houses and Dockyard Wall, Ancient Monument

C1720. The main entrance to Morice Yard, and one of the most attractive small entrances to any Royal Dockyard. The actual gateway is formed by two heavy granite pillars with small ornamental mortars mounted on top. Above the roadway is a large lantern supported by scrolled ironwork. To the north and south of the pillars are the two houses, which may date back to the foundation of the Ordnance Yard. They both have two storeys and basements, heavy stone plinths and pitched slate roofs with gables at their north and south ends. Both are stuccoed.

Morice Gate, Plymouth

Adjacent to the gateway is some of the oldest surviving Dockyard Wall also dating from c1720. It is built of a mixture of rubble and shale with very heavy pilaster buttresses of the same material. The wall has a pitched top with slate covering.

No 4 Store, Morice Yard, Plymouth

No 4 Store, Ancient Monument

1722. One of the oldest surviving stores in any Royal Dockyard. Of brown shaly stone, eleven bays long, two storeys, attic and a hipped roof with flat top. Granite plinth and, above the first floor a low parapet. A fine collection of lead rainwater heads with GR 1723 cast onto one. The building is still in use as a store and the interior is little altered from the original.

No 8 Store, Ancient Monument

1722. Similar in design and size to No 4 Store. Eleven bays, two storeys and a later addition. The building is partly covered by cement rendering and is still used as a store.

No 8 Store, Morice Yard, Plymouth

No 2 Store, Ancient Monument

C1730. The west building of two attached buildings to the south of Store No 3, facing north and built of dunstone. Two storeys, high plinth, rough string course and a hipped slate roof. Seven bays east-west by three bays north-south. Most of the original sash type windows. Several internal features of interest including an unusual king and queen post roof construction.

No 2 Store, Morice Yard, Plymouth

PLYMOUTH

HM NAVAL BASE MORICE YARD

No 16 Store, Morice Yard, Plymouth

No 16 Store, Ancient Monument

1743–44, the former Gunpowder Magazine, the second to be built in the Morice Yard. Constructed of stone rubble it has a central section breaking forward with four red brick pilasters and a pediment over. Below the pediment is a cartouche of the Duke of Montagu (1688–1749), who was Master General of Ordnance 1739–1749. Between the outer brick pilasters are two narrow brick-edged vertical loops. The central double door is copper sheathed. On either side of the central section are two segmental-headed windows with intact glazing bars. Above is a crudely repaired stone-capped parapet. The corners of the building have red brick quoins. Barrel vaulted interior, partly supported on massive brick piers.

No 2 Store, Ancient Monument

Dated 1776 on rainwater head. The east of two attached buildings to the south of store No 3 was originally a small workshop. Two storeys, five bays with sash windows all with original glazing bars. Ashlar walls in grey limestone, rusticated quoins, plinths, string course, cornice and parapet. Interior has traces of original domestic layout.

No 5 Store, Morice yard, Plymouth

No 12 Store, Morice Yard, Plymouth

No 12 Store, The Painted Canvas Store, Ancient Monument

Dated 1777 on rainwater head. A small workshop, once the twin of No 2 Store but now used as a store. Two storeys, five bays and south facing. Rusticated quoins, floor banding and dressed stone window surrounds. In poor condition.

No 17 Store, Ancient Monument

C1790. Adjacent to Store No 16 and connected by a short covered way, this is a single storey building of coursed dunstone rubble with brick dressings and a hipped slate roof. The west front has four sash windows set in recessed brick arches; the south end has a small semi-circular headed doorway. Interior with unlined walls and cement floor.

Colour Loft, No 5 Store, Ancient Monument

C1840. Erected probably for use as a gun carriage store. Three storeys in random-sized ashlar limestone. Seven bays east-west by three bays north-south. Roof at west end is hipped, but the east end has a pedimented gable carrying a clock. Most of the original glazing bars survive intact and within is a fine double stairway. The building is now used as a store and is in good condition.

No 6 Store, Morice Yard, Plymouth

Sail Loft, No 6 Store, Ancient Monument

C1811. Two storeys, in ashlar with plinth, string courses and hipped slate roof. Ground floor windows round-headed, those on the first floor are segmental, all with modern metal frames. The interior on the ground floor exhibits traces of its original use. The building is now used as a sail loft.

No 3 Store, Ancient Monument

C1812. Similar in design and contemporary with Sail Loft No 6, however the interior has been more extensively altered. On the ground floor wooden pillars have had to be partly replaced by steel girders and some modern partitioning has been inserted. Many of the windows still have their original glazing bars.

The North Gate, Ancient Monument

C1860. A pleasant mid-Victorian dockyard entrance, on a smaller scale than most. Two large piers with rusticated pilasters, cornice and stone-ball ornaments on top, flank the entrance way. Over the roadway is an ornate iron lantern supported from the piers by scrolled iron-work. The outside faces of the piers have doorways in them with semi-circular heads in which are elaborate open ironwork tympana with VR motifs. Behind the doors, brick vaulted passages allow for pedestrian access. The main gates are modern. The gateway is set back from the line of the dockyard wall and connected to it by short curving walls, each containing five firing loops. Inside, to the west is a single storey police office in granite, with hipped slate roof, plinths and cornice. The central door is flanked by two windows.

NORTH YARD

The Quadrangle, Ancient Monument

C1845–57. An enormous quadrangular group of buildings erected to provide facilities for Queen Victoria's new steam navy. Of monumental construction this is the finest and most complete group of Victorian dockyard development to survive relatively unaltered. The most important features are the north, south and west facades. Designed by Barry and G T Green.

Police Offices

C1850, limestone with granite dressings, comprising two distinct elements. The south part is one of two towers with cupolaed turrets which were linked by a quadrant screen and archway forming the original entrance to North Yard. The clock was transferred from the other tower when it and the screen were demolished when the Frigate Refit Complex was built. The northern portion is less monumental in style.

ROYAL NAVAL HOSPITAL, High Street, Stonehouse
MOD (Navy), Freehold

Begun in 1758 and opened in 1762. By Alexander Rovehead, architect, probably with William Robinson as consultant. A series of buildings laid out on axial lines, which is the earliest example in England of a hospital with a limited number of patients in each block in order to prevent contagion. *UCHB*.

Trafalgar Block, Grade II*, Group Value

Three storeys and attic with windows in a 1:3:1 pattern. In stone rubble with ashlar dressings including first floor banding and plain architraves. The centre projects boldly with a pediment containing a lunette over a three-light second floor window above and an arch containing a Venetian window. Three arches to an open passageway on the ground floor. Central cupola and turret, hipped roof of new interlocking tiles. The interior is very plain with a plain central staircase, no other internal features are of interest. The Trafalgar block originally contained the chapel.

Sundial in front of Trafalgar Block
Grade II, Group Value

An 18th C sundial made by John Gilbert of London. On a turned stone pedestal standing on what is said to be a millstone made of six stones dovetailed together.

Ward Blocks, Grade II*, Group Value

Ten blocks forming a square and connected by Tuscan colonnades in granite, now mostly glazed and with an upper corridor built over. Like the Trafalgar Block these ward blocks are also in stone rubble with ashlar dressings. Three storeys high and generally five windows wide. Parapet with band, two bands to first floor and plain architraves. Sash windows in reveals. Hipped roofs with new interlocking tiles.

Pay Office and Admiral's Office
Grade II, Group Value

Part of the original hospital plan. Two small single storey and attic blocks with three arches facing inwards towards each other, with three openings at the sides. In stone with rusticated quoins and a parapet. Slate mansard roofs with central chimneys. The Admiral's Office has a lead rainwater pipe and head dated 1765.

Residences Nos 4, 5, 6 and 7
Grade II, Group Value

1765. Built as official residences with a brick facade now cement rendered. Three storeys, attics and basements. Twelve windows with the centre six breaking forward slightly with a wide pediment over. Parapet. Slate mansard roof with dormer lights. Banding. Later sash windows without glazing bars. Three porches, the centre porch is double, with fluted pilasters and pediments, glazed doors and sides. Plain area railings.

Residences Nos 11, 12 and 13
Grade II, Group Value

18th C. In stone rubble with ashlar dressings. Slate roofs. The centre block, Number 13, has two storeys and an attic and is three windows wide. Slate mansard roof with end chimneys, parapet and wide pediment with attic lunette. A first floor Venetian window with blocked flanking lights. At ground floor the later addition of an enclosed porch, rendered. Two small dormer lights.

Nos 11 and 12 are flanking wings to No 13 at the centre. Again two storeys high and three windows wide but with slate hipped roof behind a parapet. Central wooden porch with fielded panels and glazed sides and door. Wide cornice. Continuous banding at first floor level. All the windows are sashes with glazing bars.

North Gateway and Store
Grade II, Group Value

18th C, in stone rubble with ashlar dressings. Corrugated iron roof with gabled ends. Two storeys high. Parallelogram on plan with key blocked archway through the centre on a parallel axis. Eight windows with plain architraves with reveals in line with the axis of the building. The central archway breaks forward slightly with large iron gates to the outward end leading to the jetty where the patients were landed. The rooms over were stores for hair and bedding.

Landing Jetty, Grade II, Group Value

18th C. A short jetty of rusticated granite projecting into Stonehouse Lake (now reclaimed land), used originally for landing patients from the ships. There are landing steps at each side of the jetty.

The Water Tower, Grade II, Group Value

18th C. The original water tower for supplying the hospital. Octagonal on plan and constructed in stone rubble with ashlar quoins and dressings. Circular openings, one or two on each side. A brick round arch opening on the ground floor, now blocked. A low pitched roof with central octagonal turret with lead-clad dome with ball finial.

Boundary Wall along Clarence Place and Stoke Road
Grade II, Group Value

1758 to 1762. A long stretch of stone rubble wall on the south and east side of the Royal Naval Hospital. Approximately 15′ high and intended to prevent the desertion of patients who were usually recruited by press-gangs.

Water Tower, Royal Naval Hospital

Residences Nos 8 and 9, The Medical Mess
Grade II, Group Value

1806 by Edward Holl. Two almost identical blocks in ashlar facing each other and forming a square with Nos 4, 5, 6 and 7. Slate hipped roof with wide eaves. Three storeys, attics and basements. Nine bays. Sash windows without glazing bars with flat arches over. Continuous banding at first floor level and again at first floor sill level. No 8, the north block, has a central semi-circular porch with Tuscan columns and entablature, a glazed curved door with flanking windows between columns. The south block or Medical Mess has a later glazed porch in the centre and four round headed dormers at roof level.

Medical Mess, Royal Naval Hospital

The Inner Gate-Piers
Grade II, Group Value

Early 19th C. Reputed to have been designed by Daniel Alexander (1768–1846). Rusticated stone piers with pedimented cap over carved relief and fretted band. After removal one of the piers has been replaced.

PLYMOUTH   ROYAL NAVAL HOSPITAL

Main Gate and Gate-Piers
Grade II, Group Value

Victorian. Large ashlar gate piers with cornices and rusticated ball finials. Studded and panelled wooden gates with openwork cast iron panel bearing the Royal Arms. Flanking railings curved outwards to cast iron lamp standards; the lamps are modern. Originally there was a cast iron overthrow between the piers.

Main Gate, Royal Naval Hospital

Octagonal Posting Box, South of the Pay Office
Grade II, Group Value

Made 1853–59. A private posting box used only by the Royal Naval Hospital but probably cast by one of the Post Office contractors. It does not bear the lettering 'Post Office', nor 'Letter Box', nor the Royal cypher. In cast iron, painted red, in the form of an octagonal pillar with angle beading, topped by a flat moulded cap and on a moulded base with shallow plinth. Vertical posting slit with external flap.

Chapel, Grade II, Group Value

1883 in the gothic revival style. Rubble. Slate roof with dormers and a wooden clerestory with trefoil lights. Wide two-light aisle windows with depressed arches with carved chevrons. Porch at the west end and above it a large nave window with two round headed cusped lights. Low tower on south west corner with octagonal stone spire. Semi-circular apse at the east end.

Chapel, Royal Naval Hospital

PLYMOUTH

ROYAL CITADEL, Hoe Road
MOD (Army), Freehold
Ancient Monument

A very fine example of late 17th C fortification, begun in 1665 to the design of Sir Bernard de Gomme. It was intended to overawe the town which had held for Parliament in the Great Rebellion as well as protect it from external agression. The pentagonal bastioned trace is fairly regular towards the Barbican and the Hoe but follows the irregular shape of the ground towards Fishers Nose. The limestone rubble faced rampart survives up to the granite cordon on all sides and much of the embrasured parapet is intact, particularly the western part. Hoe Road follows the line of the ditch with the covered way still traceable beyond it. The Mound perpetuates the ravelin protecting the main gate.

The main gate dated 1670, is a curiously untutored exercise in French Baroque style. The lower stage, corresponding in height to the rampart, has a low archway flanked by paired Ionic pilasters with swagged capitals. The upper stage has an almost semi-circular pediment over the centre and two Corinthian columns related to nothing in particular framing an almost frivolous central niche. The pediment houses the Royal Arms and there are carved trophies on the sides of both stages. The sally port in the west curtain is a much simpler and plainer but effective composition.

The interior accommodation was largely rebuilt in the late 1890s but there are several surviving 17th C buildings, though much altered. *AMS, Pevsner.*

Governor's House

C1670, enlarged shortly after completion, rebuilt in 1903. Three storeys and attic, coursed limestone rubble with granite quoins and window head string courses. Paired sash windows, two fine semi-circular headed granite doorways. Deep bracketed eaves to slate mansard roof with dormers.

Governor's House, Royal Citadel, Plymouth

Royal Citadel, Plymouth

Storehouse, Royal Citadel, Plymouth

Storehouse

C1670, three storeys, limestone rubble with granite window head string courses. Sash windows, blocked four-centre headed granite doorway. Slate roof behind parapet.

Royal Chapel of St Catherine

Rebuilt 1845, on a Greek cross plan with galleries in three of the arms. Coursed limestone rubblew with ashlar dressings. Grouped and simple traceried two light windows, reused 17th C granite doorway. Slate roof with coped gables.

The principal Victorian buildings are substantial limestone blocks with gabled slate roofs which form an imposing group. The largest block has been unfortunately sited on the line of the north east curtain. In front of the main block is a lead statue of George II in Roman military dress of 1728, rather lost in the expanse of the parade ground.

King George II, Royal Citadel, Plymouth

Main Block, Royal Citadel, Plymouth

PLYMOUTH

Bull Point House, Kinterbury Road
MOD (Navy), Freehold

An early 19th C two storey rendered and painted square house, three bays by two, with a first floor level band course. Mainly 12 pane sash windows, with two French-windowed single storey canted bays on adjacent sides. Hipped slate roof on 'U' plan, ornamental cappings to brick chimney stacks. Crude attached porch. To one side is a yard between a lower service wing and a detached rubble coach house and stable block.

Bull Point House, Plymouth

Kinterbury House, Kinterbury Road
MOD (Navy), Freehold

Early-mid 19th C two storey and attic rendered and painted house, three bays by two. Rusticated angle strips, plain surrounds to 16 pane sash windows. Added timber porch. Deep boxed eaves to hipped slate roof with dormers.

Kinterbury Villa, Kinterbury Road
MOD (Navy), Freehold

Dated 1901 over the entrance. Square two storey squared limestone rubble house with a hipped slate roof. Demeaned by a lean-to glazed porch.

Kinterbury House, Plymouth

MANADON HOUSE, Royal Naval Engineering College, Manadon Hill
MOD (Navy), Freehold
Grade II

The house has a complex building history which has not been fully elucidated. Probably early 17th C, perhaps on the site of an earlier building, but much altered later in the century when the front elevation acquired its present character. Two storeys and attic, limestone rubble with granite dressings, slate roofs.

Seven window entrance front, the windows converted from cross-mullion and transom to sashes. Continuous hood moulds over the windows. Very deep bracketed timber eaves with coresponding scrolled gable kneelers, dormers with alternately triangular and segmental pediments. Moulded arched granite doorway, now within a Tuscan porch.

Three projecting wings at the back, the centre one containing a fine 17th C oak staircase rising to the top storey. The part of the east wing adjacent to the front range was pushed out and given sash windows with 'gothic' glazing bars. Service stairs have been inserted in the spaces between the wings which have themselves been extended and the space between them partly built up and a tribune formed on the main staircase.

The interior contains fine 17th C granite doorways and fireplaces, not necessarily all in their original position, and 17th C panelling and doorcases, particularly on the first floor which was then the principal storey.

On the north side of the rear yard is a rubble out building of indeterminate age with a granite arched doorway of unsophisticated character. A large walled kitchen garden lies to the north east.

Manadon House, Plymouth

Stables, Grade II

C1800, north east of the house and now attached to the east wing. Stone rubble with segmental brick arches to windows. Projecting centre with elliptical brick arched carriageway and attic with Diocletian window. Slate roof.

Stables at Manadon House

Chapel, Grade II

C1800, immediately north of the house, formerly a barn. Nine tapered circular rubble piers down each side supporting the slate roof, now infilled mainly with glazing. Converted in 1961 to the design of Robert Potter.

Cottage

Two storey slate roof rubble cottage west of the chapel. Three bay south elevation with massive buttresses and two-centre headed windows.

Gate Piers, Grade II

A pair of rusticated granite piers sited well away from the house to the south west and marking the entrance to the original drive. Fitted with modern metal gates.

PLYMOUTH

Millbay Pier Tower, Plymouth

Mount Batten Tower, Plymouth

Millbay Pier Tower
Customs and Excise, Leased

Three storey octagonal limestone tower. Arcaded ground stage with cornice on rusticated piers. Granite lintels to sash windows on first and second floors, blind on alternate faces. Eaves cornice and parapet. Circular stair turret attached to one face.

Raglan Barracks Gateway, Military Road
Devonport
MOD (Navy), Freehold
Grade II

1853 by Captain Fowke, RE. A monumental block in austere classical style, squared limestone rubble with granite dressings, plinth, entablature and blocking course. Tall central vehicular archway flanked by low pedestrian arches, set within a shallow portico of Tuscan columns on attached pedestals, with the Royal Arms carved in the tympanum of the pediment. Two stage central clock and bell turret with cupola and weather vane. Very plain architraves and bracketed cornices to blocked windows in wings. The only surviving building of the barracks which have been replaced by married quarters. *UCHB*

Mount Batten Tower, Mount Batten Point
MOD (RAF), Freehold
Ancient Monument, Grade II

Built in 1665 to complement the Royal Citadel guarding the entrance to the Cattewater and Sutton Pool, then the heart of the port, and named after Captain Batten, Governor of Plymouth during the Civil War. A stout cylindrical three storey rubble tower surmounted by a gun platform carried on the vaulted roof behind an embrasured parapet. *AMS.*

Raglan Barracks Gateway, Plymouth

PLYMOUTH

MOUNT WISE, Devonport
MOD (Navy), Freehold

Hamoaze House, Grade II

Formerly Admiralty House, built in 1795 for the
Duke of Richmond but considerably altered since.
Limestone ashlar with cornices and blocking
courses. Three storey centre with two storey wings.
Enclosed porch with round-headed doorway and
side windows, absorbed in later first floor glazed
verandah. Hipped slate roof; iron area railings.
Good quality side door to George Street. *UCHB.*

Admiralty House, Grade II

1820, formerly Government House. Limestone rubble with ashlar dressings, quoins, first floor band
course, cornices and blocking courses. Three storey
centre with two storey wings. Semi-circular porch
with added outer porch, flanked by tripartite sash
windows in arched recesses. Hipped slate roofs.
UCHB

Hamoaze House, Plymouth

Admiralty House, Plymouth

Mount Wise House, Grade II, Group Value

At the east end of George Street. Early 19th C painted stucco three storey five by six window block. Rusticated segmental arcaded ground floor with impost band. First and second floor sill level band courses, bracketed first floor window cornices. Cornice with stepped parapet; hipped slate roof. Added glazed porte-cochère. *UCHB*.

Mount Wise Hard Landing Steps, Grade II

1820. Double flight of granite steps with iron railings curving up from the jetty to a central weatherboarded pavilion on a battered stone base. A further straight flight of steps leads to an archway in the wall of Richmond Walk with VR 1847 inscribed on the keystone. *UCHB*.

Mouth Wise House, Plymouth

Mount Wise Hard Landing Steps, Plymouth

PLYMOUTH

Mount Wise Cottages

Paired 19th C coursed limestone two storey houses, three windows wide with tripartite sashes flanking their central doorways. Hipped slate roof.

Captain Scott Memorial, Grade II

A winged bronze figure surmounting a tall stone base of diminishing tapered stages, with bronze reliefs of Scott's journey to the South Pole and medallions of the expedition members.

Mount Wise Cottage, Plymouth

Custom House, Plymouth

Custom House, The Parade
Customs and Excise, Freehold
Grade II*, Group Value, Conservation Area

1820 by David Laing. Two storey, five bay symmetrical facade of granite ashlar. Plinth, rock faced rustication to ground floor with cornice at first floor level. A three arch arcade to centre of ground floor flanked by similar segmentally headed openings. This entrance loggia has a three-bay groined vault.

Round-headed first floor windows in sunken panels, impost banding. Cornice and parapet, with centre section of the latter raised with clock face. Royal Arms below first floor central window. Hipped slate roof. *UCHB*

PLYMOUTH

HMS DRAKE ROYAL NAVAL BARRACKS
Saltash Road, Devonport
MOD (Navy), Freehold

Clock Tower, Royal Naval Barracks

Prior to 1853 crews were paid off at the end of each commission. After the introduction of continuous service accommodation was initially provided in hulks which proved most unsatisfactory. The naval barracks at Devonport was the first to be started, in 1879, and provided the model for those later built at Portsmouth and Chatham. It was much enlarged subsequently and has been partly rebuilt since the war but the original layout and the important buildings are intact.

The original buildings are squared local limestone rubble with Portland stone dressings and slate roofs. The rigidly rectilinear layout is relieved by the fall of the ground towards the river and tree planting. *UCHB.*

Clock Tower, Grade II

A most amazing edifice of great elaboration. Surrounded by a colonnade of paired columns, now enclosed with glazed screens. Clock tower rising in diminishing stages with stepped or splayed angles. Massively bracketed balcony above clock face level with cast iron balustrade and similar balustrade above. Plainer wing projecting to the south.

Main Gates, Grade II

Large iron gates between two pedestrian archways set within vermiculated rusticated pilasters supporting segmental pediments. Wider than when originally built.

Main Gate, Royal Naval Barracks, Plymouth

Wardroom, Royal Naval Barracks, Plymouth

Wardroom, Grade II

Three storey centre and linked flanking blocks with rusticated lower storey. Projecting central entrance tower with Ionic porch approached by divided staircase, surmounted by a tall stone domed cupola with a ship weathervane. Bracketed stone balconies with pierced balustrades on flanking blocks. The staircase hall, bar and coffee room have elaborate beamed ceilings on scagliola columns with alabaster columns. The wardroom has unusual wooden reliefs of naval engagements in silhouette against the upper part of the walls between the panelling and the roof trusses.

Drill Shed, Grade II

Two low wide parallel aisles separated by columns, with low pitched steel truss roofs, enclosed within monumental Portland stone walls, only the plinth and parapet being local limestone rubble. The front towards the parade ground is relatively plain with nine bays of segmental headed windows separated by rusticated pilasters either side of the pedimented central entrance. The angles are treated as turrets with blind arches and pedimented attics. Each side has two massive entrances with rusticated Tuscan columns supporting segmental pediments.

Drill Hall and Howard Blocks, Royal Naval Barracks

PLYMOUTH   ROYAL NAVAL BARRACKS

St Nicholas, Royal Naval Barracks, Plymouth

Church of St Nicholas

Actually orientated south-north so that the apsed sanctuary rears impressively over an undercroft accommodated in the fall of the ground which extends under the flanking Lady Chapel and organ chamber. Wide eleven bay nave with low narrow aisles stopping one bay short of the 'west' end and with porches at either end. Apsidal baptistry projecting from the 'west' end.

The exterior is characterised by buttresses of two splayed faces meeting at right angles which form complex groups of facets at the angles. The 'eastern' part has round headed lancets and the 'western' windows with simple semi-circular tracery. There is a triple bell-cote over the chancel arch. Slate roofs to nave and sanctuary.

The interior is plain with Portland stone dressings to painted plaster walls. The aisles have quadrant vaults and the nave an open timber roof with arch-braced kingpost trusses. The sanctuary has a timber vault.

Drake House, Royal Naval Barracks

Drake House

An attenuated irregular block, three storeys and attic, with canted bays and steeply pitched slate roofs with panelled barge boards. Cast iron balconies and fronts to projecting window sills.

Other surviving Victorian buildings include Seymore Block and the matching north half of Howard Block, which form with the Main Gates, Clock Tower and Wardroom Block a group on Quarter Deck Road, and Frobisher Block and the theatre. Raleigh, Grenville and Exeter Blocks are survivors of the original barrack blocks.

93

PLYMOUTH

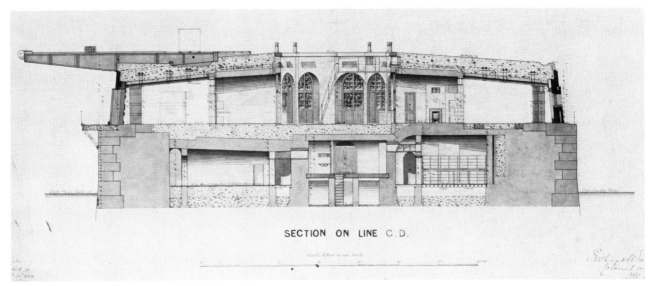

Breakwater Fort, Plymouth Sound

Breakwater, Lighthouse and Fort, the Sound
MOD (Navy), Freehold
**Fort Ancient Monument, Breakwater and
Lighthouse Grade II**

The breakwater was begun in 1811 under John
Rennie and completed by his son Sir John in 1840.
It is over a mile long in the centre of the Sound
with its ends splayed inwards. The lighthouse at the
western end was completed in 1844.

The fort was built on the recommendation of the
1859 Royal Commission on the defence of the United Kingdom to close the Sound against unwanted
intruders. Oval in plan, 144 by 114 foot, sited on
Shovel Rock behind the centre of the breakwater.
The design was changed during construction from
four tiers of granite casemates with iron shields to a
single armoured tier of 18 guns above a masonry
base. The fort was completed in 1870 but not
armed until 1879. It was unique among the English
sea forts in having its guns on muzzle-pivoting car-

riages, which permitted smaller less vulnerable gun-
ports but whose development caused considerable
delay. It was made redundant by the construction of
Penlee Point and Renney Batteries in 1894-95
armed with breach-loading guns which could command the whole approach to the Sound from dry
land. *UCHB, Hogg.*

Fort Staddon, Staddon Lane
MOD (Navy), Freehold
Ancient Monument

The highest position in the south eastern defensive
system of Plymouth, built on the recommendation
of the 1859 Royal Commission. On a symmetrical
pentagonal plan with the face and flanks enfiladed
by caponiers and a defensible 'keep' in the gorge.
Intended solely for land defence but never armed.
Now used as a signal station. *Hogg.*

Fort Staddon, Plymouth

SALCOMBE

54 Fore Street
Customs and Excise, Hired
Grade II, Group Value, Conservation Area

Probably early 19th C. One of a pair, the whole stucco facade being three storeys high and four windows wide. Two modern shop fronts, floor bands, sash windows with glazing bars and a wide eaves soffit. Hipped slate roof over. *UCHB.*

TIVERTON

4 St Paul's Street
Department of Transport, Hired
Grade II, Group Value, Conservation Area

Probably built in the mid 19th C by John Heathcoat as an industrial housing scheme, together with St Paul's Square to which this street leads. Basically a continuous terrace of two storey, three window houses in pinkish brick on either side of the street. Sash windows with glazing bars. Arched doorcases with rusticated jambs and archivolts in patent stone, radial bar fanlights and four-panel doors. Slate roofs in the dormers and brick chimney stacks. No 4 has been rebuilt in more recent times. It is only two windows wide and the doorcase has been re-used to screen altered construction behind. The dormer window has been omitted. *UCHB.*

WEMBURY

Fort Bovisand, Bovisand lane
Leased, MOD Freehold
Ancient Monument, Area of Outstanding National Beauty

Basically two forts; the earlier, Staddon Point Battery was built in 1847 to replace Staddon Heights Battery of c1770. Its masonry casemates were retained as a barracks and linked to and enclosed in the ditch of Fort Bovisand proper which was built to the south on the recommendation of the 1859 Royal Commission. There is an arc of 24 massive iron shielded granite casemates, intended to have two tiers but completed in 1870 with one. The interior fittings of the casemates are intact. Superseded with the construction of Penlee Point Battery Various 20th C excrescences on top. Leased to the Fort Bovisand Underwater Centre. *AMS, Hogg.*

Watch House Battery, Bovisand Lane
MOD (Army), Freehold
Ancient Monument, Area of Outstanding Natural Beauty

Late 19th C. a small redoubt linked by rock-cut ditches to Fort Staddon to the north and Fort Bovisand to the South. *AMS, Hogg.*

Renney Battery
MOD (Navy), Freehold
Area of Outstanding National Beauty

Built with Penlee Point Battery across the Sound c1895 to supersede The Picklecombe, Breakwater and Bovisand line of forts closing the entrance when breech loading guns supplanted rifle muzzle-loaders. An open battery with magazines below and accommodation sunk in the rear. *Hogg.*

BOVINGTON

Bovington Farm House
MOD (Army), Freehold
Grade II

First half of the 18th C, two storeys and attic, T-shaped plan. Red brick above a rubble plinth, thatched roof. The entrance front is a symmetrical five window composition with a central entrance. First floor level band course. Flush sash windows with keystoned heads, segmental on the ground floor. The rear wing has been rebuilt and the interior of the main block remodelled; to the north is a large extension of only slightly later date. *RCHM*.

Bovington Farm House

BRIDPORT

45 South Street
Department of Employment, Part Hired
Grade II, Conservation Area

An 18th C, former net factory; two storeys of coursed rubble, with a slate roof. *UCHB*.

CATTISTOCK

Chantemarle
Home Office, PSA Freehold
Maintained by Home Office
Grade I, Area of Outstanding Natural Beauty

A building of several periods, of modest size but considerable importance, the whole being of much greater interest than the sum of the parts. The oldest part of the house is the C 16 wing at an angle on the west side of the main range, its flint and rubble work contrasting with the later Ham Hill ashlar.

The central block is dated 1612 on the keystone of the porch doorway. It was built for John Strode by Joseph and Daniel Rowe of Hamadon (ie Ham Hill) to a design by Gabriel Moore, on an "E" (for Emmanual) plan. The projecting wings have gone, if they were ever completed, and the attic gables, but the porch retains its oriel window and classicising entrance; otherwise the arched heads of the windows are remarkably archaic.

Somewhat decayed in 1910 it was skilfully restored for F E Savile, who added the service wing to the north and linked the pre-existing block of 16th C date to the south by the stair hall. The gardens were beautifully and sympathetically set out at the same time by Inigo Thomas.

Little survives of the early interiors except the original Chapel but the Jacobean style plaster ceilings executed in 1910 are fine if not almost too grand. Further alterations were made by E J Warren after 1919 for C H St John Hornby and the gardens extended. In 1950 it was acquired for a Police Training Centre and further accommodation built in the grounds. *UCHB, RCHM, Pevsner, Colvin, Country Life*.

CHRISTCHURCH

Stable/Barrack Block, MVEE, Christchurch

MILITARY VEHICLE EXPERIMENTAL ESTABLISHMENT
Barracks Road
MOD (Procurement Executive), Freehold

The barracks were built in 1795 as part of the first organised programme of barracks building, which ended in a welter of corruption and accusations. Built as a Cavalry barracks and later used by the Royal Artillery and the Royal Engineers, the remaining original buildings are important historical survivals. *UCHB.*

Stable/Barracks Block, Grade II

Two storeys and attic, with a basement under the south end. Nine bays by three with the end pairs of bays broken forward slightly. Gauged brick arches, mainly segmental but semi-circular on the ground floor ends, with plastered tympana over mainly triple sash windows with glazing bars. Hipped slate roof with lead dressing. Numerous slate-sided lead-topped dormers with sash windows with glazing bars. Chimney stacks on ridge line.

The interior completely belies the regularity and symmetry of the exterior. The south end was self-contained on the ground and first floors; in the central section all the structural partitions fall across windows and the partition does not correspond with the break in the external walls at the north end.

Two if not three bays of the ground floor were originally stabling and retain the cast iron columns supporting the first floor which formerly divided the stalls. The doors and windows have been much chopped about to meet changing requirements. The attic is open virtually from end to end with groups of flues arching over. The roof is carried on a series of massive queen-post trusses, more or less regularly placed along its length with little regard to the disposition of dormers or first floor windows.

Guardroom, Grade II

A dainty single storey building. Red brick with burnt headers and gauged brick flat arches to sash windows with glazing bars. On the front is a portico of six slender Tuscan columns. Hipped slate roof surmounted by a timber clock turret and arched bell-cote with a lead capping and weather vane.

Guardroom, MVEE, Christchurch

CHRISTCHURCH

PSA Works Office

Single storey, red brick with burnt headers. Gauged flat arches to sash windows with glazing bars. Hipped slate roof. A former married quarter, it is the only relatively intact survivor of the U-shaped ranges which ran around the perimeter of the original site.

Officers' Mess, **MVEE**

1876, two storeys, red brick with buff brick and some Portland Stone dressings. Slate roof. A small building in a chapel-like style, delightfully sited on a terrace over looking the River Stour.

Officers' Mess, MVEE, Christchurch

40 High Street
Manpower Services Commission, Hired
Conservation Area

With No 38, a late 19th C two storey building with a narrow central bay flanked by wide side sections. The ground floor shop fronts are separated by a dentil cornice from the painted stucco first floor. String course at impost level of the round headed multi-light windows with margin paned sashes. Moulded cornice and high parapet in front of hipped slate roof.

DORCHESTER

The Keep, Bridport Road
MOD (Army)
Grade II, Conservation Area

The gatehouse to the infantry barracks, the only section of the two former barracks still in MOD occupation, it houses the Dorset Military Museum. Built in 1876–77, possibly by Major A C Seddon. A four storey pitched faced Portland stone tower in Hollywood medieval style, crowned with a crenellated parapet on a corbel table. Round stair turrets on the front angles rise above the general level, linked by a corbelled stone balcony at first floor level, with spirally stepped loopholes on the rear elevation. There is a circular 'caponier' with a conical stone roof attached to the northern corner. *UCHB.*

The Keep, Dorchester

Southern*

LULWORTH

St Andrew's Farmhouse
MOD (Army), Freehold
Grade II, Area of Outstanding Natural Beauty

C1700. Two storeys in coursed rubble with dressed quoins. A long rectangular plan of five bays with a central gable porch. Three brick chimney stacks, the end ones set diagonally over stone coped gable ends. The house was extensively altered internally in the mid 19th C and most of the extensions and out houses to the rear were added at the same time. Original features still survive in the west gable end in the form of blocked moulded stone mullioned windows at first floor and attic levels. The former window is however without the mullion. In more recent times the building has been re-roofed in red tiles which is unfortunately totally out of keeping with other buildings in the vicinity or indeed this part of the county. To be rehabilitated as PSA offices. *UCHB, RCHM.*

Barns at St Andrew's Farmhouse

Two 17th C barns, the larger of nine bays with stone walls and the roof carried on jointed-cruck trusses, the other of brick and stone with a later tiled roof. *RCHM.*

St Andrew's Farmhouse, Lulworth

POOLE

18 Market Street
Department of Health and Social Security, Hired
Grade II, Conservation Area

Dated on a tablet on the rear wall inscribed SV 2 May 1797 and on an adjacent rainwater head; extended at the back in the mid 19th C. A typical town house of the period, three storeys, basement and attic. Three window brick front with painted floor level band courses, cornice and parapet. Gauged brick flat arches to sash windows with glazing bars. The ground floor windows have been replaced since RCHM by a bowed shop window. Fine doorway with an open pediment on attached Doric columns and elaborate fanlight. *UCHB, RCHM.*

99

POOLE

Custom House, Poole

20 Market Street
Department of Health and Social Security, Hired
Grade II, Conservation Area

A mid 18th C substantial merchant's mansion house. Three storeys and cellars, five window front, unevenly spaced. Brick, with cornice and parapet, gauged brick flat arches with stepped keystones to sash windows with glazing bars. Central doorway with fluted pilasters and pediment. The rear elevation is carefully composed around the staircase windows. The staircase has a fine balustrade and much original panelling remains in the upper floors. *UCHB, RCHM.*

Custom House, The Quay
Customs and Excise, Leased
Grade II*, Conservation Area

A reconstruction after a fire in 1813 of the earlier Custom House of c1788 which was itself a rebuilding of the Red Lion Coffee House. A foursquare but not clumsy three storey Georgian brick pile with a hipped slate roof. Almost domestic in character except for the pair of curved flights of steps up to the Tuscan porch on the principal, first floor, modelled on those of the Guildhall. The porch is surmounted by a Royal Arms of more recent date in cast iron. *UCHB, RCHM, Pevsner.*

PORTLAND

HM NAVAL BASE, Castletown
MOD (Navy), Freehold

The anchorage at Portland was designated a harbour of refuge in 1844 and planning of the southern breakwaters began the following year. The Verne Citadel, now HM Prison, was planned in 1857 to defend the moorings and the 1859 Royal Commission on the Defence of the United Kingdom recommended additional precautions. By 1870 a coaling and watering depot had been established and in 1892 Portland was designated a dockyard. The northern breakwaters were constructed between 1893 and 1902 to give protection against torpedo boats as much as the elements. *UCHB, RCHM, Hogg, E A Andrews and M L Pinsent: 'The Coastal Defences of Portland and Weymouth', Fort 9 Supplement.*

Inner Breakwater, Grade II

Portland stone, 1700 feet long with a casemated back face. At the shore end of Prince Consort Walk (over the casemates) is a plaque with the Royal Arms commemorating the laying of the foundation stone by Prince Albert in 1849 and the final stone by the Prince of Wales in 1872. Designed by J M Rendell and built by the Royal Engineers with convict labour. There is a small fort designed in 1859 for eight 68 pounders at the South Ship Channel end.

Outer Breakwater, Grade II

Completed in 1872, by J M Rendell and J Coode. Mainly Portland stone, 6,400 feet long with much later dumping and accretions. There is a small fort at the South Ship Channel end.

Breakwater Fort, Grade II

At the northern end of the outer breakwater though built as an independent structure. Recommended by the 1859 Royal Commission, one of the series of great armoured sea forts, the others being at Spithead and Plymouth. Completed in 1875 and intended to be armed with fourteen 12·5 inch rifled muzzle loading guns.

Former Dockyard Railway Station

The railway reached Portland in 1865. A range of mainly two storey Portland stone buildings of varied elevational treatment with mullioned windows and a profusion of gables. Sandwiched between the Castle Road and the now abandoned railway it is used as the MOD Police Office.

Jetty Storehouse

The most imposing building in the dockyard, grandly sited freestanding on the jetty. A massive Portland stone block of rubble with ashlar dressings, articulated by pilaster strips and plate bands. The long sides have an arched opening in each bay with very limited openings above. There are large arched entrances in the end walls and semi-circular windows in the western gables, the eastern ones having been rebuilt in brick. The timber trussed 'M' roof is now clad in corrugated asbestos cement sheet and the interior has been much altered.

To the south of the store house are two minor buildings of good quality Portland stone ashlar used as a foundry and a store. In front of these the kerb line of the filled in graving dock is still visible.

Jetty Storehouse, HM Naval Base, Portland

PORTLAND

East Weare Batteries

Forming the outer defences of the east side of the Verne Citadel, 200 feet above. Earth batteries constructed by 1850 were replaced by 1870 with the present concrete and masonry emplacements, subsequently much altered and enlarged. The five batteries completed survive in various states of dereliction.

East Weare Detention Barracks

On the hillside behind the batteries. A low rectangular Portland stone block built around a courtyard, with flankers on two diagonally opposite corners.

Master Gunner's House, Portland Castle
MOD (Navy), Freehold
Ancient Monument

Portland Castle is one of Henry VIII's series of coastal defence forts and is in DOE guardianship with the main building open to the public. The 17th C stables and brewhouse on the west side of the castle yard were converted and enlarged to form the Master Gunner's house in the early 19th C. This is now a two storey block with rendered walls, crenellated parapet and windows with timber mullions and labels. The west wall is built over the original yard wall. *RCHM.*

TYNEHAM
MOD (Army), Leased
Site of Special Scientific Interest

St Mary's Church, Grade B

The former parish church, cruciform in plan with a central stone double bellcote, built of rubble and ashlar with stone tile roofs. The nave and north transept are of medieval origin, not later than c1300. The church was restored in 1744 when the west wall was rebuilt. In the early 19th C the chancel arch and arch to the north transept were rebuilt and enlarged, the south transept being rebuilt towards the middle of the century. The south wall of the nave was also rebuilt with the possibly 14th C south porch taken down and rebuilt as the west porch. Benjamin Ferrey was responsible for part at least of this work. The chancel is more recent.

The interior still contains a few of the original fittings, though most were dispersed to surrounding places of worship when the village was evacuated in 1943. The church is now used as a visitors' information centre. *UCHB, RCHM.*

Tyneham Manor, Grade II

1567–83, by Henry Williams, fronting an earlier 14th C wing and with some later additions in the 19th C. Most of the house has now unfortunately been demolished, however the original south west wing, dating from the 14th C still survives. This was the original hall but has been divided by a cross wall and chimney stack, having a rebuilt 16th C segmental-pointed stone arch over the fire place, and by an inverted floor reached by a winding stone newel stair. Part of an open truss over the hall remains and also the timber-framed partition between the hall and service rooms, and the closed truss above it. The open truss has an arched-braced collar beam, the arch braces being cusped and supported on hammer beams, and there is a cusped infilling above the collar; only part of this truss survives. The closed truss has the remains of two doorways, presumably to service rooms, flanking a central post, and to the north behind the later stair are the posts for a taller doorway which may have led to a staircase, under tie beam and collar beam are curved braces and two small struts form a 'V' above the collar. Under the purlins are arched wind braces, the lower ones cusped. *UCHB, RCHM.*

Rectory

Mid 19th C. Now reduced to the state of a safe ruin. Originally two storeys high. Stuccoed walls with stone dressings and low-pitched slate roofs. Rectangular on plan with four bays to each elevation except the north, which has a small re-entrant to give light to the staircase. The doorway to the east has a flat stone hood carried on scrolled brackets. The windows had double hung sashes. *RCHM.*

TYNEHAM
Site of Special Scientific Interest

Post Office Row

A row of cottages which incorporated the village post office. In the vernacular, originally with roofs of thatch but re-roofed 1880 with stone slates. The row has been partially demolished and the walls 'capped off' reducing the whole to the status of the safe ruin. The external precast concrete telephone box still remains. To the north west of Post office Row is the old School House which dates from 1860 and consists of a single room, 28 foot by 15 foot. This building has recently undergone restoration works and has been re-roofed in stone slates.

Lutton Farm, Crown List

Late 17th C or early 18th C. A two storey house in a ruinous and dangerous state. The barn to the west of the house dates from the 17th C and comprises seven bays with the roof carried on jointed-cruck trusses with roughly arch-braced collar beams. *RCHM.*

North Egliston Farm

Probably dating from the 18th C. A row of cottages and farm buildings grouped around the farmyard. The cottages are in rubble, with stone slated roof and later brick chimney stacks. Individual stone porches with round-headed openings and some with the original stone slated roof.

WEYMOUTH

84 The Esplanade
Department of Health and Social Security, Part Hired
Grade II, Conservation Area

68–84 The Esplanade are the seventeen surviving houses of the eighteen which originally made up Royal Terrace, begun c1816. Three storeys, basement and attic, the three houses at each end being broken forward and built slightly higher than the intermediate ones. Nos 82–84 have been rendered and painted. *UCHB, RCHM, Pevsner.*

Custom House, The Quay
Customs and Excise, Freehold
Grade II, Conservation Area

An early 19th C three storey Georgian brick building, with a delightfully dynamic composition of pedimented stone doorway, Royal Arms and square and bowed bays, which is a vital part of the waterfront scene. There is a fine Long Room on the first floor. The roof is supported on composite king-post trusses over the second floor which was formerly an undivided storage area, with internal and external hoists surviving at the rear. *UCHB, RCHM.*

Custom House, Weymouth

BATTLE

The Old Guild Hall, 34a High Street
Ministry of Agriculture, Part Hired
Grade II, as part of 34

A two storey building with an 18th C front. The ground floor is stuccoed between modern shop fronts, the first floor tile hung with straight and scalloped courses. Sash windows with glazing bars on the first floor, with a canted bay on the corner. Half-hipped tiled roof, with a parapet on the main elevation. It occupies a prominent position at the head of the High Street. Beneath are vaulted cellars which were once part of the medieval hall of the Mountjoy Guild. *UCHB.*

BRIGHTON

St Anne's House, 49 Buckingham Place
Customs and Excise, Department of Employment, Freehold
Grade II, Conservation Area

Probably c 1820. A tall four storey house with a five window painted stucco front, dentil cornice at third floor level, cornice and parapet. Cast iron balcony at first floor level; sash windows without glazing bars. Porch with Greek Doric columns in antis. There is a later two storey extension to the west. *UCHB.*

The Old Cottage, South Road, Preston
Customs and Excise, Leased
Grade II, Conservation Area

Forms part of a single building now divided into three parts. Dated 1636 on the front but has more the appearance of an 18th C farmhouse. Two storeys with a two window front, flint with red brick dressings. Doric doorcase with pediment to semi-circular headed doorway with fanlight. There are later additions on the east and west sides. *UCHB.*

St Anne's House, Brighton

The Old Cottage, Preston, Brighton

BRIGHTON

Army Records Store, Ditchling Road
MOD (Army), Freehold

Built in 1854 as a Diocesan College, dated over the door and on the rainwater heads. Two and three storey building of several ranges in impoverished ecclesiastical gothic style. Knapped flint walls with ashlar dressings. Mainly plate traceried windows, some oriels, and some bar tracery with hood moulds. Numerous gables and dormers. Steeply pitched tiled roofs; the chimney stacks have been cut down. What the building gains from its prominent position it loses by the uninspired modern additions at the back.

Army Records Store, Brighton

EASTBOURNE

Martello Tower No 66, Langney Point
Coastguard, Leased
Ancient Monument, Grade II

1806, part of the system of coastal defence against invasion from Napoleonic France. Two storey circular brick tower. Parapeted gun platform carried on a ring vault on the central pillar. Vaulted magazine in the basement; the remainder of the intermediate floor is timber. *UCHB, Sutcliffe.*

Martello Tower No 66, Eastbourne

HASTINGS

ORE PLACE
MOD (Army), Leased

Dated 1863 on the porch, a medium sized mansion on a splendid site on high ground overlooking the town and the Channel. Two storeys, coursed Wealden sandstone rubble with ashlar dressings, bracketed cornice and blocking course. The pitched roof has been replaced by an asphalt flat leaving the chimney stacks standing up baldly. Three window centre to entrance front, flanked by canted bays, with large central porch with coupled Tuscan pilasters, entablature and balustrades.

Large entrance and staircase hall with tiled floor. The house was extended and later became a Jesuit seminary with large additions of no architectural merit. In the grounds are a small summer house and a farm yard constructed of massive sandstone ashlar blocks.

Ruins of Ore Manor, Ancient Monument

The pathetic remnant of the medieval house, demolished when the present mansion was built.

LEWES

Crown Court, 182 High Street
Lord Chancellor's Department, Freehold
Grade II, Conservation Area

1808–12 by John Johnson, built as the County Hall. Five bay three storey Portland stone front with the end bays slightly projecting. Two bays were added on the right hand side and the side bays of the ground floor colonnade filled in in the 19thC. Heavily rusticated ground floor, balustraded panels in front of the tall first floor windows. The three window panels in the centre of the second floor contain Coade stone figures of Wisdom, Justice and Mercy. A fine console cornice with a blind attic over the centre bay. This is a very distinguished building in a most important street.

RYE

Custom House, 7 High Street
Customs and Excise, Part Hired
Grade II, Group Value, Conservation Area

A two storey 18th C house with a three window patched red brick front. Small timber door case with a flat hood, six-panel moulded door. Double modern shop window to the west of the door. Timber eaves cornice to the tiled roof. The side towards Conduit Hill has two half-hipped gables and is tile-hung above the ground floor. There is a large added block at the back forming an 'L' with the original house. *UCHB.*

Eagle House, Landgate
Department of Employment, Part Hired
Grade II, Conservation Area

A late 18th-early 19th C house with a two storey three window front. Red brick with stuccoed window heads, first floor sill level band course and cornice. Sash windows with glazing bars removed and the semi-circular head over the doorway has lost its fanlight. Hipped tiled roof behind the parapet. *UCHB.*

TELSCOMBE

Telscombe Manor

TELSCOMBE MANOR
Lord Chancellor's Department, Leased
Grade II, Group Value, Area of Outstanding Natural Beauty

16th C in origin, much altered and extended in the 18th and 19th Cs. A very picturesque and irregular composition. Two storeys and attic, flint and render, with mullioned casements and sash windows. Gabled tiled roofs with dormers. At the back a 19th C circular flint tower. *UCHB.*

Manor Cottage, Grade II, Group Value

Stuccoed 18th C two storey three window cottage. Horizontal sliding sash windows, tiled roof, modern porch.

Manor Barn, Grade II, Group Value

18th C, flint with red brick dressings, half hipped slate roof.

CHELTENHAM

94 All Saints Road
Department of Transport, Hired
Conservation Area

Late 19th C, in stucco. Two storeys, basement and attic, and three bays wide. Moulded banding at plinth and again at first floor level. Wide dentil treatment to banding below deep soffited eaves. Hipped slate roof with two dormer lights. Single glazed sash windows at ground floor level with cornices over supported on inverted consoles. Slightly more elaborate treatment to first floor windows including console support to sills and fleur-de-lys decoration to lintels. Single storey link to the adjoining property on the right, with steps up to the main entrance in a decorated round-headed opening.

John Dower House, Crescent Place
The Countryside Commission, Leased
Grade II, Conservation Area

Early 19th C in ashlar. Four storeys over a basement and eight windows wide, sash with bars. Delicate wrought iron guards to the first floor windows. Floor banding, cornice and parapet. Roof not visible. A central stucco Ionic porch with coupled columns and entablature with sculptured Royal Arms above. The garden railings are intact. *UCHB*.

County Court, Regent Street
Lord Chancellor's Department, Freehold
Grade II, Conservation Area

Dated 1870 and in the Italianate style. Two storeys in ashlar, with a rusticated ground floor and quoins above. A five window front to Regent Street with modillion cornice and balustraded parapet. To County Court Road, a facade with a three window central bay with the entrance to the left and a single window wing to the right. There is a fine apsed end, with a first floor window, beyond the entrance. Graeco/Egyptian porch with paired square and round columns. Good cast iron railings with lion-head finials on the main stanchions. *UCHB*.

John Dower House, Cheltenham *County Court, Cheltenham*

GLOUCESTER

31 Commercial Road
MOD (Army), Freehold
Grade II, Group Value, Conservation Area

Formerly the Custom House but now the museum of
the Gloucestershire Regiment. Early 19th C in the
classical style. An ashlar faced building of two storeys
with five windows grouped 1:3:1. Plinth, elongated
chamfered quoins and a central porch which projects
slightly with a simple entablature, cornice and high
plain parapet which forms a balustrade before the first
floor central window. Banding at first floor level and
again at first floor sill level. First floor sash windows
with architrave surrounds and hood cornices over.
Simple cornice and parapet at high level with carved
Royal Arms centrally overall. *UCHB.*

31 Commercial Road, Gloucester

Probate Registry, Gloucester

Probate Registry, Gloucester

Probate Registry, Pitt Street
Lord Chancellor's Department, Leased
Grade II

Dated 1858. By Fulljames and Walter. A delightful one
and two storey gothic building in coursed rubble with
dressed quoins and red tile roofs. Oriel windows and
one eight-light window with trefoil heads. Gables and
clustered chimneys. *UCHB.*

Shire Hall, Westgate Street
Lord Chancellor's Department, Hired
Grade II, Group Value, Part Conservation Area

The original building was designed by Sir Robert
Smirke in 1816, of which the Westgate Street facade,
with a recessed giant Ionic portico, and the polygonal
Assize Courts at the rear now survive. The building
was altered considerably between 1844 and 1896 and
was extended in 1909–11, with extensive modern
additions in 1966. *UCHB.*

NAILSWORTH

Glenholm, George Street
Ministry of Agriculture, Fisheries and Food, Hired
Grade II, Group Value

Early 19th C. Three bays, three storeys and a basement in coursed rubble with stone dressings. Cotswold stone roof behind a moulded cornice and blocking course. Glazing bar sash windows. Central doorway with Tuscan columns, cornice and pediment. A six-panel door, the upper four being glazed. Wrought iron railings partly survive to the left of the door. Within, the original staircase with a ramped handrail. *UCHB*

Millbrook House, George Street
Department of Employment, Hired
Grade II, Group Value

Early 19th C. A two storey ashlar front with moulded cornice and blocking course. At first floor level, four 19th C sash windows in pairs. Below, a late 19th C shop front to the left with the central entrance and house entrance incorporated. A late 19th C Tudor arch doorway in a square surround to the right of centre, then a 1:4:1 light bay to the right with moulded heads and transoms to its lights. *UCHB*

QUEDGELEY

Manor Farmhouse, RAF Quedgeley
MOD (RAF), Freehold
Grade II

15th – 16th C. Originally a moated manor house with parts of the circuit still in existence. Half timbered structure with fine carved wood hammer brace roof timbers as well as an excellent moulded oak beam ceiling on the ground floor. Externally the building is partly roughcast, over the timber framing, and partly brick faced with a c1810 wing in stucco with a pedimented porch. Tiled roof. *UCHB*

Manor Farm, Quedgeley

SOUTH CERNEY

Control Tower, South Cerney Airfield
MOD (Army), Freehold

Late 1930s. In brick with steel framed windows. A two storey, three bay frontage with the centre bay recessed and rising a further storey to form the main control room. Octagonally faced clock on all four sides. A functional and crisp building with its simplicity worthy of note.

Control Tower, South Cerney

ALDERSHOT

ALDERSHOT GARRISON
MOD (Army), Freehold

Until the establishment of 'The Camp at Aldershot' in the mid 19th century there was no permanent camp or Garrison in the country suitable for a large scale concentration of troops for training or exercise. Following the establishment of a temporary training and exercise ground at Chobham, which had largely been instigated by the Prince Consort, a permanent site for such activities was chosen at 'Aldershott'. At that time a small forgotten hamlet, surrounded by miles of forbidding and desolate heathland, and the haunt of highwaymen. The terrain was ideal for manoeuvres.

A small party of Royal Engineers set up camp near the village in 1853 to survey the area prior to the War Office preparing plans for development. The men were to be accommodated in timber huts and 1600 of these were erected in two 'camps' north and south of the Basingstoke Canal. In March 1854 war broke out with Russia and the regular troops having been shipped out to the front their accommodation was filled with reserves, militia and reinforcements. It was realised at this time that permanent barrack accommodation would be needed, and an unparalleled and ambitious programme of building was instigated, completed in 1859. These were the famous 'lines' of barrack blocks in a stark military classical style and included the numerous support buildings needed to accommodate the largest concentration of troops in the Kingdom. An immensely impressive and unique development of military architecture. They were entirely demolished during the 1960's, and their various ephemeral remains lie scattered around the garrison in the form of odd pediments and plaques.

The Prince Consort took an active part in the design and layout of the new 'Camp at Aldershot' and it was he who suggested the building of a residence for the Queen during visits to the Camp. He chose the site and approved the design for the 'Royal Pavilion'. Royal visits became a regular feature of life at Aldershot and continued until present times. Some spectacular parades and reviews were held in their honour.

This permanent station of Army life began to enlarge rapidly, the War Department acquired lands stretching from Woking to Fleet, and the camp began to take on the appearance of a military town. The village of Aldershot expanded to provide civilian services to the forces.

Men and equipment were mobilised and despatched from Aldershot for every major conflict from the Crimean War to the Falklands campaign, usually via the camp's own military rail terminal which was surrounded by the 'Field Stores' complex. In 1914, the Regular Army being despatched abroad, Aldershot became a major training establishment. Between the

wars it became headquarters for the 1st and 2nd Divisions, and as the 'Aldershot Command' continued its training role. The Second World War saw intensification of training with the greater part of the barracks becoming the UK base for the Canadian Army. After the war Aldershot continued – to this day – as a training centre for the national Army; and is home station of the Regular Battalions of the Parachute Regiment and HQ of the Airborne forces.

Despite the rapid advances in military thought, and the extensive alterations and demolitions to the original accommodation, a large number of historically and architecturally important buildings remain within the Garrison. Only one of the original timber buildings remains, and alterations for modern operational requirements have ruined others, but neglect coupled with careless and insensitive minor works are potentially most dangerous to the remains of the military heritage at Aldershot.

The northern part of the Garrison is actually in Farnborough but is described here for completeness. The buildings were mainly erected within a period of 50 years and are spread over a considerable area which warrants the description of a military town, so they are described in street rather than chronological order for ease of reference. Some buildings of lesser but not negligible interest are noted in an appendix to this section. *UCHB, Pevsner, Lt Col H Cole: 'The Story of Aldershot'.*

Aldershot Garrison in 1866

Beaumont Barracks Riding School, Aldershot

Beaumont Barracks Riding School, Alexandra Road
Grade II

C 1854–59. The last remaining building of the Beaumont Cavalry Barracks complex and virtually all that remains of the once extensive ranges of cavalry accommodation throughout the camp. A massive rectangular block providing a clear span of 180 foot by 60 for the riding school, the last remaining of three similar buildings, and one described by a contemporary guide book . . . "in point of size and accommodation reputed to be the finest in England".

Beaumont Barracks Riding School, Aldershot

The building fell into disuse following the introduction of mechanisation in the Army, and has survived due to the efforts of a few who realised its value as an important piece of military heritage which could still be used. The tan was restored after the last war; and although not entirely suitable to modern methods of horse training, the building in which Sir Winston Churchill received his training before being shipped off to South Africa and the Boer War once again resounds with the sound of horses' hoofs and the shouts of command.

Balloon School Memorial, Alison's Road
Grade II

A small metal plaque on concrete base commemorates the foundation of the School of Ballooning formed as a branch of the Royal Engineers in 1892 on this site. The first interest in aerial warfare in Aldershot, and which led eventually to the foundation of the Royal Aircraft Establishment at Farnborough.

Pediment from Warburg Barracks, Alison's Road
Grade II

C 1857. Royal Coat of Arms carved in high relief in Portland Stone. Set on a base of brick paviors in a garden setting. Originally within the central pediment of the Officers' Mess of the East Cavalry (Warburg) Barracks.

ALDERSHOT   ALDERSHOT GARRISON

Cavalry Brigade Veterinary Lines, Auchinleck Way

Mid 19th C. The remains of a once huge range of
stabling, primarily used as the veterinary centre for the
cavalry brigade. Much has been demolished, but
beside ranges of stabling, the operating theatre and
recovery boxes remain. Also several loose boxes retain
their original sling beams and cast iron fodder baskets.
An original forge is still in use, and the picket lines are
now used as stores. Along Wellington Avenue are the
remains and ruins of stable and cart yards, forges and
other ancillary accommodation including a wagon
ramp.

Veterinary Lines, Aldershot

Royal Garrison Church, Aldershot

Royal Garrison Church, Aldershot

Royal Garrison Church of All Saints
Farnborough Road
Grade II

1863 by P C Hardwick. The Church was once an
important landmark of the camp, its tower, with
pyramidical roof, 121 feet high dominating the area. It
was known almost immediately after its completion as
the 'Red Church' (the name falling into disuse with
modern political connotations) due to the red bricks
from which it was built. When new these must have
been a vivid contrast to the yellow stocks and grey slate
of the other buildings. In those days it was a far more
conspicuous landmark than to-day. Trees have been
allowed to obscure it, and modern development making it impossible to see except at close quarters.

It is however, arguably the finest building
architecturally in the Garrison, and is a truly imposing
composition. Some vigorous but strong detailing, but
without fuss, and cleverly massed to give complex
elevations from each aspect. A simple triple roof
structure, the nave defined by greater height, ending
in gables. The chancel projects, and north and south
elevations have gabled porches. Small vestries add to
the organic feel of the architecture. The redbrick is
relieved by stone tracery and dressings.

The interior is dominated by a high circular window
at the east end, but its main historic features are the 80
or more memorials on its walls, and inlaid in the walls
commemorating famous battles and brave deeds of
Army men. High above hang old Colours of famous
regiments.

ALDERSHOT

Anglesey House, Aldershot

Anglesey House, Farnborough Road
Grade II

C 1860. Built as a residence for the Commander of the Cavalry Brigade, and probably named after the First Marquis of Anglesey who commanded the whole of the Cavalry and Artillery under Wellington at Waterloo. It later became the residence of the Deputy District Commander.

A severe irregular brick house of two storeys with a minimum of decorative features. The interior has been converted to offices and the Court Martial Centre.

Royal Pavilion Guard room, Farnborough Road
Grade II

1855. The last remaining building of the Royal Pavilion complex, and the only original timber buildings remaining from the 'Camp at Aldershot'. The Royal Pavilion was demolished in 1962 and the lodge and stables in 1971.

The guardroom, a small single storey verandahed building, in the style of the Royal Pvilion, is now in a sorry state, its roof felted and in need of refurbishment; it is used for storage.

Royal Pavilion Guardroom, Aldershot

ALDERSHOT GARRISON

Vine Cottage, Aldershot

Vine Cottage, Farnborough Road
Leased to Hampshire Building Preservation Trust

C 1850. Originally the senior Royal Engineers Officer's residence, and one of the first officer's residences built in 'The Camp'.

An old cottage in the grounds of Vine Cottage was known as 'Bagman's Castle' – supposedly the home of Dick Turpin, who claimed many victims on this eerie and lonely stretch of road.

The cottage is quite plain and unspectacular save for a most remarkable conservatory, built as a lean-to along the south end of the house and rising through the full height of the building. This houses a magnificent mature vine which is now tended by a local wine-making circle. The interior has a small staircase to an upper gallery to harvest the higher branches, and the heat build-up is regulated by a series of massive sliding sashes in the glazed roof.

Willems Barracks Entrance, Farnborough Road
Grade II

1856. The remains of a gateway complex to a barracks for a brigade of cavalry, and of a pattern found in several other former barracks entrances. The front wall only is complete and now stands incongruously beside a busy roundabout fronting a council housing estate, it bears no relationship to either. A central vehicle arch is flanked by two smaller pedestrian arches, and above these are two stone plaques similar to those now sited outside Princes Hall (q.v.). Some wrought iron railings, also salvaged from demolished barrack blocks, surround the piece. Originally a guard room complex would have been immediately behind this entrance front. (A similar gateway – that to Beaumont Barracks – survives further along the road, with the remains of its guard rooms now undergoing restoration. This one was sold for development of the land adjoining.)

ALDERSHOT   ALDERSHOT GARRISON

Willems Barracks Entrance, Aldershot

Old Union Poor House (Workhouse), Hospital Hill

C 1630 in origin. An important building having both general and military historical significance which has suffered ever decreasing circumstances.. The building was originally a sub-manor or minor residence of Sir Richard Tichborne, Lord of the Manor of Aldershot. Its name at this time and subsequent history is lost until the building was acquired under the terms of the 1834 Poor Law Act by the Farnham Union as a 'Union Poor House' (Work House). It later became a school for pauper children.

In 1854 it was one of five buildings in the area purchased by the War Department for the purpose of developing the Camps, and was used until 1879 as No 2 Station Hospital. Later it became the District Pay Office.

There have been many alterations and additions to the original building. In 1838–40 a large Jacobean style two storey wing was built or adapted from the original house leaving virtually only a rear wall and the chimney stacks as original. In 1907 there was a major fire and the building was to be demolished until it was discovered that the original deeds purchased by the War Office contained restrictive covenants which required the building to be rebuilt in its original form. All this, coupled with its use at present as South Camp Community Centre and the poor condition it is in, make it very difficult to ascertain the true nature of the building. There can be no doubt of its architectural and historical value, both military and civil. It is a building which would repay greater study and which demands a considerable measure of care and attention.

Old Union Poor House, Aldershot

ALDERSHOT   ALDERSHOT GARRISON

Cambridge Military Hospital, Hospital Road
Grade II (Main Block only)

1873–79. Purpose-built military hospital, with an extensive range of wings and ward blocks. The main front block is a most imposing and monumental structure in military classical style with pedimented projecting wings of pilasters above a rusticated base and plinth; and a massive square tower in the centre. The tower is 109 foot high and is a competent and novel, though somewhat eclectic, composition. Well articulated, with its various elements altering their shape and size to emphasise and enhance the verticality, and culminating in a square clock turret with concave pyramidal shaped roof.

The clock tower originally housed the Sebastopol Bell (q.v.) which was hung to form a chime with two smaller bells cast by Gillett, Bland & Co. of Croydon in 1878.

The ward blocks behind are of utilitarian brickwork and have been subjected to a variety of alterations over the years. Fortunately at least two of them retain what appears to be their original 'day-room' elevation, one of timber frame glazing and one with a once open loggia of columns rising through two storeys.

The interiors throughout have been altered continually over the years, but the exteriors, especially the main block have survived well. A totally inappropriate and insensitive storm-porch and covered way seriously mars the architectural integrity of the main block front.

The building, and the tower especially, form a prominent and well known local land mark of some considerable importance.

Cambridge Military Hospital Mortuary Chapel

C 1900. This tiny unassuming shed-like structure conceals one of the greatest artistic treasures of the county. The chapel is panelled in a dark stained simple style and terminates beneath a frieze of breathtaking coloured gesso running round all four sides of the room, the work of Mary Watts, widow of G F Watts one of the foremost 'Arts and Crafts' group artists. She executed them in her 70th year, assisted by her 'Potters Art Guild' as a memorial to the fallen of the Great War.

They owe their miraculous survival largely to the fact that the building is very little used, and their delicate and highly fugitive colouring has been preserved by very low light levels. The only fading to have occurred is immediately opposite the entrance door where a section of the frieze receives direct daylight when the entrance door is opened. A fine allegorical and religious work of art of national importance.
Pediment from Willems Barracks, Knollys Road
Grade II

Sebastopol Bell, Hospital Road
Grade II

A bronze bell in an open wooden frame structure with hipped shingled roof, cast by Nicholas Saintain of Moscow (date unknown). The bell was one of a pair from the Church of the Twelve Apostles, Sebastopol, which were brought home with other trophies from the Crimea. (The second bell was hung in the Round Tower at Windsor Castle.)

This bell was sited adjacent to the Time Gun on Gun Hill, and a sentry, posted at the old Headquarters offices near this point would stroke the hours upon it. When the Cambridge Military Hospital (q.v.) was built, the bell was hung in the tower, where it remained until 1961, when it was taken down on the instigation of the Garrison Commander, by a party of Royal Engineers. The present framework which closely resembles the original, was erected for it outside the District HQ facing Queen's Avenue. It was moved again in 1978 to its present site which is very near its original position on Gun Hill.

Cambridge Military Hospital, Aldershot

ALDERSHOT

The Prince Consort's Library, Knollys Road
Grade II

1860. Designed by Captain Francis Fowke, RE (designer of the Royal Albert Hall and the 'Cole' wing of the Victoria and Albert Museum). Built at the instigation of, and paid for by the Prince Consort. The books and librarian's salary were also provided from the Privy Purse until the 1930's. Probably one of the best examples of military architecture in the Garrison, and certainly the least altered. A design of clearly intended superiority to the very largely functioned buildings which surrounded it, though not in the least ostentatious. The detailing is crisp and restrained, with its minimal ornamentation of terracotta dressings and pattern brickwork. A stone plaque in the front gable bears the Arms of the Prince Consort.

Internally the library has timber framing and panelling, fitted bookcases, and a gallery running around three sides. The contemporary furniture and prints on the walls give it the air almost of a gentlemen's club. Minor alterations to form offices have not destroyed the fireplaces and staircases etc. A rare survivor indeed.

A lecture hall was built on in 1911 for use of the Aldershot Military Society who also provided money for purchase of books for the library. This is now used as the main lending library.

Prince Consort's Library, Aldershot

Willems Barracks Pediment, Aldershot

Pediment from Willems Barracks, Knollys Road
Grade II

C 1857. Adjoins the Library on the north side, probably intended to form a stop to the view from Knollys Road, past the library buildings. Consists of a carved Portland stone coat of arms formerly set within the Pediment in the centre of the Officers' Mess of West Cavalry (Willems) Barracks. Now assumes an entirely two-dimensional appearance, and is unimaginatively set-up. Probably highlights more than any similar surviving piece of architectural ephemera the meaninglessness of such conscience-saving gestures and the regrettability of the demolition of the buildings to which they were attached in the first place.

Lille Barracks Main Block, Lynchford Road
Grade II

C 1890. An unpretentious military building, in red brick, long symmetrical front with minimum of architectural articulation. The interiors very plain and unostentatious. One of three such surviving buildings of the period, and of typical form. (The other two being at Tournay Barracks and McGrigor Barracks.

Canal Bridge, Aldershot

Canal Bridge, Queen's Avenue
Conservation Area

An interesting cast iron bridge over the Basingstoke canal at the point where a pontoon had been built by Royal Engineers in 1854 to connect North and South Camps. Strengthened to take road traffic, the balustrades, torchières, and handrails down to the canal have survived well. The bridge is now barely perceptible to road traffic, and probably goes unnoticed by most pedestrians.

ALDERSHOT   ALDERSHOT GARRISON

Fox & Maida Gymnasia, Queen's Avenue
Grade II

The first gymnasium in Aldershot was built in 1861 following a War Office decision that soldiers' training should be extended beyond that of formal drill and weapons, and that the physical aspect of the soldier's education be improved. The Army Gymnasium Staff was formed and led eventually to the foundation of the Army Physical Training Corps of today.

The Fox Gymnasium was built in 1894 to replace the small gym. of the 1860's, and was known as the 'Big Gym'.

The two gymnasia, and the Boxing Centre (formerly the Albuhera Drill Hall) are all built in similar style of red brick with simple slated roofs over large span light metal trusses. They all have very distinctive arched corbelling at their gable ends.

Fox is the largest, and has a gabled porch to the south flank, and extensive outbuildings. It is also the most important historically, and other buildings near-by are architecturally interesting.

Maida is smaller, and has three wings added, but despite some modern work to the west side, remains the least altered of all three gymnasium buildings.

The Observatory, Queen's Avenue
Grade II

1906. A small circular rotunda of brick with domed roof, the entrance steps having curved flank walls with a stone coping terminating with a ball finial. Inside is a 9 inch refracting telescope presented to the 'Aldershot Army Corps' by one Patrick Alexander, a resident of Mychett and local amateur astronomer.

Observatory, Aldershot

St Andrew, Queen's Avenue

1927 by Sir Robert Lorimer. The most important inter-war period building in the Garrison. It stands on the site of the old 'Iron Church' moved here in 1866 from Thorn Hill and demolished in 1926. (One of the original three commissioned by the Board of Ordnance.) It was decided to build a Church of Scotland after the 1914–18 war as a memorial to Scotsmen who had fallen in the conflict. Sir Robert Lorimer, one of Scotland's greatest architects, was chosen. Buildings south of the Border by Lorimer are scarce, and those in brick are scarcer still. This church – one of Lorimer's last major works – shows how perfectly well he appreciated the qualities of that medium.

The building has a simple and very strong form, with virtually no unnecessary ornament other than red brick dressing used to harmonise gently with the walls of greyer brick. A most interesting element, and trademark of Lorimer was the subtle use of the round tower, recalling antecedants among numerous Scottish castles, but unfortunately now taken down.

The interior is very plain and business-like. There is some stained glass and few memorials, beneath a coffered roof which occupies almost the whole area. The joinery of pulpit, altar and organ case are conventional and are the only elements that distract from "The superb simplicity of this Hall."

It was opened in 1927 by HRH The Princess Royal, but was far from complete, additions were made to the structure in later years. *Country Life*.

St Andrew, Aldershot

ALDERSHOT   ALDERSHOT GARRISON

St Michael and St George, Queen's Avenue
Grade II

1892 designed by Maj. Pitt and Lt Mitchie, as St
George's Garrison Church. As a result of replanning
of Garrison Churches in 1973 it became Garrison RC
Church of St Michael and St George. St Michael is
taken from the previous RC Garrison Church of St
Michael and St Sebastian.

A large red brick church with a tall tower which has
become an easily recognisable landmark in the Camp.
An austere building with a minimum of Portland stone
dressings and devoid of any ornament save some
interesting brickwork over the main (west) entrance.
The interior is cavernous, of yellow brick, and in a
stripped gothic style, with a gallery above the West
door. There are numerous stained glass windows and
memorials. The carved oak lectern and pulpit were
originally used in the 'Iron Church'.

The Swimming Bath, Queen's Avenue

1900. Designed by Col the Hon John Napier, CMG.
Napier was appointed 'Inspector of Gymnasia' in 1897
and, after an unsuccessful attempt to convince the
Army to provide a swimming pool, he used nearly
£12,000 of funds from the Royal Tournament for the
purpose. Prior to the construction of this pool the men
had to use the Basingstoke Canal or Cove Reservoir as
bathing facilities.

The building is one of the hidden delights of
Aldershot being screened from the road by trees. It has
a highly whimsical appearance with the entrance
through a glass covered lean-to porch into a galleried
entrance hall beneath a dome. The entrance hall is
marred by a totally unsuitable paint scheme and poorly
placed partitions, notice boards and other im-
pedimenta. The main baths area is spanned by an iron
trussed roof with some delightful detailing, and has an
apsidal end. A building deserving of greater care and
attention than hitherto received.

Wellington Monument, Round Hill
Grade I

1846, sculpted by Matthew Coates Wyatt. The most
important single monument in the Garrison. The
bronze statue is three-times life-size and is intended to
represent the Duke of Wellington as he appeared at
Waterloo, mounted on his favourite horse –
Copenhagen. (There was considerable public argu-
ment as to whether or not the Duke did actually sit for
the sculptor . . .). The statue has an interesting and
unusual history.

St Michael and St George, Aldershot

Funds were raised by public subscription for the
statue largely at the instigation of a Mr Thomas Bridge
Simpson, who formed the 'Wellington Military Memorial Committee' in 1838. They raised £14,000. It was
proposed to erect the finished statue on top of Decimus Burton's Triumphal Arch at Hyde Park Corner,
immediately opposite Apsley House (the Duke's London home) and formerly an entrance to the gardens of
Buckingham Palace. There was fierce public debate
about the siting which was eventually approved by
Parliament after a full size wooden model had been
erected on the arch.

Controversy over the siting of the statue continued
after its placing, and any suggestion for its removal was
taken by the Duke as a personal slight. The arguments
finally abated shortly before the Duke died in 1852 and
were not raised again until 30 years later when a road
widening scheme necessitated the re-siting of the arch.
The statue was taken down and lay in pieces in Green
Park for some time before the Prince of Wales suggested that it be moved to Aldershot. And so, in 1885,
the statue was re-erected on a simple rectangular base
of Red Corsehill stone on the summit of a natural
mound, overlooking the Royal Pavilion and Garrison
Church, which was surrounded by an oval of upended
cannon, their exposed muzzles having metal caps to
which a continuous chain was attached. *See Back Cover*

ALDERSHOT

South East District Headquarters, Steele's Road

1895, a long red brick building in similar style to the Officers' Messes of the same date, but more distinguished architecturally. There are moulded brick details and Portland stone dressings, tall chimney stacks and an imposing entrance in a projecting centre bay with terracotta ornament and Royal Arms above. The main entrance is flanked by two old cannon, and consists of a porch formed of stone columns with a small balcony above. The exterior windows still retain their original blind boxes – a rare survival.

The interior is rather plain and office-like, save for the entrance hall, which contains a magnificent cast and wrought iron staircase. A single flight ascends to a landing lit by three large round-headed casements, then returns in two flights up to the first floor. A most unusual and distinctive feature, strictly functional, but an ornamental device very much in the tradition of military architecture. The lower entrance hall has a mosaic floor inset with the monogram of Queen Victoria and a small vestibule, immediately after the porch, which all survive intact.

Additional Buildings of Interest

Louise Margaret Hospital for Women and Children: 1898. Built during the time HRH Duke of Connaught was commanding Aldershot District, and named after the Duchess who took a deep interest in the building and its work.

Tournay and McGrigor Barracks Main Buildings; 1890s, similar to Lille Barracks (q.v.)

Wellesley House: 1890's former residence of a Brigade Commander.

Blandford House: 1890's Former residence of Major General of Administration, with some fine interiors.

Field Stores: Originally the Royal Army Ordnance Corps mobilisation stores, adjoining the Government Siding Railway Station. A rather run-down and dilapidated group of buildings, the best buildings being blocks 7 and 24.

Royal Army Medical Corps Memorial, Gun Hill: A stone and granite memorial with fine bronze sculpture by W Goscombe John. Cast by Burton of Thomas Ditton.

Gun Hill House: Well proportioned and finely detailed neo-Georgian block, with some good interiors.

Smith Dorrien House, Aldershot

Smith Dorrien House: Former Methodist Soldiers Home. Distinctive red brick building with Portland stone dressings on an important corner site.

Knolly's Hall: Originally a school for officers' children. Designed by W Bevan, one time Chief Government Architect in the Transvaal.

Memorial Chapel, Military Cemetery: 1879. A little Gothic chapel in polychromatic brickwork. Replaced an earlier wooden chapel which burnt down.

Memorial Chapel, Military Cemetery, Aldershot

Royal Army Medical Corps Memorial, Aldershot

AMPORT

Amport House
MOD (RAF) Freehold.

Amport House has a long history, the Manor of Amport being mentioned in Domesday. The manor was part of the Barony of Basing where Sir William Paulet was created First Marquess of Winchester in 1551. There is no trace of any of the earlier houses, although some documentary and archaeological evidence provides a good description of the Georgian manor of 1806. This latter house was some distance from the present one and was demolished when the 14th Marquess decided to rebuild in 1857. He chose for his architect William Burn, a leading architect of his day, responsible for some major advances in country house planning. His genius as a planner far outweighed his talents at style or design, as is apparent at Amport, the elevations being rather staid and unadventurous. Burn developed the theme of separating yet interconnecting the various functions of life in large houses. A client who employed Burn would not seek innovation or ostentation in style, but would be guaranteed every possible aspect of privacy, convenience and comfort. Amport is one of his lesser houses, but it can be seen even today that a vast amount of secondary accommodation was provided to allow comfort for what are no more than four or five principal rooms.

The last Marquess – the 15th – was killed in action in the Boer War and the house was then sold to a Mr Phillipson in 1918 and to Col. Sofer-Whitburn in 1922. The latter commissioned another great architect – Sir Edwin Lutyens – to layout the garden terraces. These have matured beautifully and show a masterly combination of formal water courses on a series of terraces coupled with informal planting and rough-cut stonework, punctuated with urns and balustrading. The whole balances the formal garden front very well by extending the symmetry, and still providing something of the organic feel of Burn's rambling plan. Lutyens also designed the entrance gates and piers, which are monumental but not of his best, and a row of thatched cottages behind the stables (no longer part of the estate). The grounds also contain some superb specimen trees.

Internally there have been the inevitable alterations and poor treatment meted-out to any such house which undergoes drastic change of use (it is now the RAF Chaplains' College) but much of interest still survives well.

The panelling in the hall was put in by Sofer-Whitburn and the stained glass to the stairs was put in in 1902, presumably copies of similar glass mentioned as being in the 1806 house. Most of the remainder is Burn, the most interesting areas being the main stairs and the small dining room or morning room (now lecture theatre) which has some superb joinery obviously taken from an earlier house.

Amport House

AMPORT

Amport House

There are still many fine examples of fireplaces, ironmongery and joinery around the house, and a fine triple-cylinder oil engine remains in pristine condition, previously used for pumping water and providing electric light.

A more obscure and distinguished combination than Burn and Lutyens it is difficult to imagine, and it is most gratifying to see this unusual house so well preserved and in active use. *Pevsner, Griouard.*

BRAMSHILL

BRAMSHILL HOUSE, Police Staff College
Maintained by Home office, PSA Freehold
Grade I

1605–12 for Lord Zouche; one of the largest, grandest and most important Jacobean houses in the country. On the site of an earlier house which has left little trace above basement level except perhaps in the shape of the insalubrious central courtyard which is little more than an air-shaft. The building history is very complex and the first main entrance on the north side was superseded by that on the south during construction.

Brick built with stone dressings, mullioned and transomed windows and pierced parapet, except on the west side which is gabled; tiled roofs and prominent brick chimney stacks. Mainly two storeys above the basement, third storey on the south front, mezzanine inserted in 18th C and attic on the west side.

The elevations are fairly austere except the centrepiece on the south entrance front which rises in superimposed orders of tapered pilasters above a loggia to a strapwork crest, with a bulbous first floor oriel. Projecting wings on this front were cut back in 1703. The east front overlooking the terrace has loggias on the ground floor of the wings; the north front overlooks the walled garden. The western service range is more homely in character.

The interiors are in keeping with the external display. The Great Hall shows this tradition in decline, confined to a single storey with the stone screen brushing the ceiling and the screens passage not aligned with the axis of the centrepiece. Above the Hall is the Chapel Drawing Room which leads to the Chapel in the south-east pavilion. More state rooms on the ground and first floors of the east range, culminating in the Long Gallery which occu-

pies the whole first floor of the north front. *UCHB, Pevsner.*

Gateway to the north of the house, Grade I.

Probably slightly earlier than the house. Brick and stone; large central arch framed with Doric pilasters and entablature with broken pediment and three obelisk finials; lower side arches with balustraded openings.

Outbuildings to the north of the house, Grade I
Brick with tiled roofs

High Bridge, Grade I

On the main entrance avenue; brick with stone balustrade and approach walls.

Gatehouse, Grade I

At the start of the main avenue. Probably 18th C; two three-storeyed turrets with caps and crenellated centre.

The house is magnificently sited on high ground with a lake at the same level and other lower down and splendid mature trees in abundance. It was bought for the Police in 1953 and the college buildings have grown into a small town, without detracting from the house.

FARNBOROUGH

ROYAL AIRCRAFT ESTABLISHMENT
MOD (Procurement Executive), Freehold

Building Q3, Grade II

Possibly 1892–93. Built as a balloon shed, for the Royal Engineers Balloon School and Factory which was then at their Headquarters in Aldershot, sited near Balloon Square (q.v.) The entire building was dismantled and re-erected on its present site in 1905–06 as a result of a Committee of Enquiry which recommended Farnborough as a better site for the launching of airships. The building was originally used for fabricating balloon and airship envelopes, its east end being partitioned off in two floors containing a storeroom at the lower level and kite room above. The western end incorporated full height sliding doors.

The basic structure of light steel frame clad in corrugated iron still remains. It is buttressed on the north side and has an outshot with additions on the south side. In 1912 it was extended, and has since been drastically altered internally by subdivision with three floors of offices. It is lined throughout with plywood and asbestos. Externally, the large doors have gone, and most of the envelope has been pierced by continuous glazing and is festooned with services. Generally in a poor condition.

One of the oldest buildings in the world continuously associated with aviation, and possibly the first to be associated with powered flying. *UCHB*.

Building R51, Grade II

1910–11. Contains part of an original portable airship shed.

Designed to be dismantled and re-erected easily, the structure consists of curved-braced iron trusses, to form the roof, supported on columns of similar design, all in sections which could be transported and bolted together to form a barrel-vaulted type structure which was then covered in canvas. (The columns are now incorporated into building Q65).

After 1914 the building was erected on its present site and covered with corrugated iron, and side aisles added, to house the Royal Aircraft Factory's foundry. The corrugated iron has since been replaced with asbestos sheeting incorporating roof lights.

A building with a highly unusual and novel structure, largely hidden by later accretions, and with significant associations with the earlier days of airship development at Farnborough. *UCHB*.

Building G1, Grade II

1910–11, a highly important building historically. Purpose built as the Headquarters of the Royal Engineers Air Battalion, ('Trenchard's HQ') which was amalgamated with the Naval Flying School to form the Royal Flying Corps in April 1912, and in turn becoming the Royal Air Force in April 1918. This is the ancestor of all RAF buildings.

The main building is two storeys, erected on the highest point to overlook the landing field. it has a simple pantiled roof, pebble-dashed walls with pilasters, and sash windows with glazing bars. A simple flat timber canopy on brackets over a rubbed brick arch adorns the main entrance door. The main elevation is ruined by the insertion of metal windows without vertical glazing bars on the ground floor; and the general appearance has been mutilated by removal of the chimney-tops, and addition of service pipes to the exterior. Internally most of the original partitions doors and joinery remains.

Adjoining is the original balloon equipment store, one storey with matching materials externally and a steel truss roof internally. Now houses the RAE museum. *UCHB*.

Building G1, RAE Farnborough

Building R51, RAE Farnborough

FARNBOROUGH　　　　　　　　　　　ROYAL AIRCRAFT ESTABLISHMENT

Building Q3, RAE Farnborough

Building G29, Grade II

C1912, one of the earliest Royal Flying Corps hangars, and probably the last surviving of its type. (The adjoining G27 building making a matching pair was destroyed in an air-crash). Known for many years as the 'Black Sheds' (though early photographs show them as white or cream) they are in a prominent position at the end of the runways, and below the HQ Building. Constructed of timber trusses with iron tension rods, and covered in corrugated iron. Originally having two pairs of large sliding doors, only one set now remains, modern folding shutter doors having been fitted some years ago. The end elevation is supported on iron buttresses, and there are numerous rear additions.

The structure has suffered due to its location, high-speed aircraft cause turbulence which has resulted in distortion of the roof members. Every truss member is now strapped-up, and numerous struts support the roof from inside. Now used as fire station and stores. *UCHB*.

Cody's Tree

A cast aluminium sculpture on stone base, on the spot where S F Cody ('Buffalo Bill') tied his aircraft to a tree to measure the engine thrust in 1908. He then went on to make the first sustained flight by an English aeroplane. The sculpture was designed and cast at RAE and incorporates the remains of the original tree.

Building G29, RAE Farnborough

FLEET

Minley Manor, Fleet

MINLEY MANOR
MOD (Army), Freehold

1858–62, by Henry Clutton, with additions and alterations by George Devey and Arthur Castings. Built for
Raikes Currie, a partner in Glyn Mills bank, who chose
the site because "he was much concerned with health;
and he had a great belief in the efficiency of gravel soil,
a high situation, and pure air . . ." Clutton had
engaged as his assistant in 1857 J F Bentley – who went
on to achieve his own fame and recognition – and
according to Bentley's sister it was he who made most
of the drawings for Minley.

Clutton was a pupil of Blore and briefly in part-
nership with Butterfield, and had published in 1856 a
lavish volume on medieval French architecture. Minley is the outstanding example of his regard for that
period and style of architecture, applied to the requirements of mid 19th C house planning. The house when
complete was considerably smaller than exists today,
but fortunately additions were commissioned from
other first-rate architects which have not detracted
from the overall concept. Raikes Currie's son, Bertram
Wodehouse Currie succeeded to Minley in 1881 and
called in George Devey (who had built a house for him
in Surrey) to add the chapel, gate lodge, stables and
orangery with its cloister. Devey died in 1886 while
work was still in progress, the Chapel being opened in
1890. Bertram Currie died in 1896 and his son,
Laurence, commissioned Devey's former assistant –
Arthur Castings – to add a large wing to the entrance
front. This he did in the style of Clutton.

The result of this conglomeration of architects is a
highly romantic and picturesque manor house of great
individuality. The interiors of the house are surpri-
singly small scale, with some elaborate decorations.
The entrance hall has a small gallery and stone floor;
the dining room has apsed ends, and the ante-room is
panelled in Spanish walnut by Mellier. The library and
passage are also richly decorated. Fortunately much of
this decoration survives intact and a number of the
interiors were photographed in the 1890's by Bedford
Lemere including the chapel which has since been
stripped of all its furniture and fittings.

Water Tower, Minley Manor

FLEET

MINLEY MANOR

Orangery, Minley Manor

The grounds were laid out by James Veitch II, the leading Victorian nursery gardener and contain a number of fine specimen trees, including 80,000 yews; informally placed beds of shrubs; a 500 yard avenue of Wellingtonias and a wisteria bower. The layout has been much simplified for ease of maintenance.

The grounds contain a number of interesting outbuildings. The most notable probably St Andrew's Church, built in 1874 by Clutton, in memory of Raikes Currie's wife. It contains some fine painted decoration and fittings. There is also a large water tower with summerhouse below by Castings. The Game Larder now contains air conditioning plant, and a charming rustic thatched summerhouse in elaborate cottage ornée style lies half-hidden among the trees near the house.

The estate has been in Army possession since 1936 and has survived well. *Pevsner, Girouard, J Franklin: "The Gentleman's Country House and its Plan".*

Chapel, Minley Manor

Summerhouse, Minley Manor

GOSPORT

Refer to the note on the Portsmouth Harbour
defences

Fort Blockhouse, Gosport

Fort Blockhouse, HMS Dolphin, Admiralty Road
MOD (Navy), Freehold
Ancient Monument, Grade II

The fort is unusual for the Portsmouth area in
exhibiting several phases of construction. It originated with a tower built in the reign of Edward VI to
hold one end of a boom across the mouth of Portsmouth Harbour. A battery was built overlooking
Spithead in 1667 by Sir Bernard de Gomme which
was incorporated as the south east front of a
trapezoidal fort built c1708–10. The landward
south west front was very strong with the gateway
in a curtain between two demi-bastions. The less
vulnerable northern fronts overlooking the harbour
were simply palisaded though with a bastion at their
obtuse angled junction. C1820 the battery was casemated and the west demi-bastion enlarged to a full
bastion. Between 1840–45 the north angle was
moved out to make the fort rectangular and the
present casemated bastion with straight flanks linked by a semi-circle built. The sea front battery was
strengthened c1850. The fort has lost its out-works
on the land front, has been riddled with openings
to facilitate traffic and is much obscured by later
buildings but is still a monument of great interest.
AMS, Williams

Monkton House, Institute of Naval Medicine
Crescent Road, Anglesey
MOD (Navy), Freehold
Grade II, Conservation Area

A mid 19th C late Regency style villa. A square
painted stucco block of two storeys, basement and
attic. First floor sill level string course, deep bracketed eaves to hipped slate roof. The western entrance front is irregularly fenestrated with a massive
central porch with coupled pilasters. The three window south front is more regular but, like the interior, is much reconstructed; it has semi-circular
dormers. *UCHB.*

Monkton House, Anglesey

No 5 Battery, Stokes Bay Lines, Admiralty
Physiological Laboratory, Fort Road, Anglesey
MOD (Navy), Freehold
Ancient Monument

A series of redoubts had been built in the 1780s to
oppose a potential landing on the vulnerable beach
west of Gilkicker Point. In the 1850s this was superseded by a continuous rampart and wet ditch between Fort Monkton and Browndown Battery, west
of Fort Gomer, which was reinforced by strong points
with casemated batteries. *AMS, Williams.*

GOSPORT

GUN BOAT YARD, Haslar Road
MOD (PE and Navy), Freehold

Transverse Slipway and Gunboat Sheds
Ancient Monument (buildings only)

Mid 19th C, for the building and repair of gunboats and later torpedo boats and other small vessels. Ships for repair were floated onto a cradle which was hauled on a carriage up an inclined slip from Hasler Lake. At the top the boat and cradle were transferred to the traversing carriage which moved them sideways to the front of the required shed or open stand to which they were finally moved. For launching the process was reversed. The cradles and carriages run on rails drawn by stationary steam engines. At its maximum extent the transverse slipway was over 1500' long with space for 50 vessels up to 120' in length on each side. The slipways were much altered during their working life. None of the original machinery survives; the original launching slip was superseded and partly filled in. The western part of the traversing pit has been filled in and built over and the eastern end built on.

Most of the south side of the transverse slipway opposite the launching slipway was occupied by covered sheds. They were built in groups of ten with rows of cast iron columns supporting light wrought iron trusses with ornamental cast iron struts at the quarter points. The groups were separated by massive brick walls and enclosed at the back. The sheds have been greatly altered at various times. The group directly opposite the launching ramp are the

best preserved. Their roofs were raised by the insertion of 5' stub columns in 1873 but the original trusses were reinstated. They retain the weather boarded gables to the cantilevered front canopies. The group of sheds to the west has been much altered and those to the east are scarcely recognisable.

At the rear are red brick workshops and the former boilerhouse and engine room for moving the ship cradles in and out of the sheds, (there was another engine house beside the inclined slip). This was used as the boiler house for the Royal Naval Hospital until recently. *AMS*

Yard Walls, Main Gate and Guardrooms
Ancient Monument

The Yard is enclosed by a massive brick wall which extends for half a mile along Haslar Road. At the corners are brick watch towers with arched windows and pyramidal slate roofs. The main gate in the east wall facing Haslar bridge is set axially with the transverse slipway. The gateway is flanked by pairs of piers with Portland stone caps and pedestrian archways between. The bases of the piers have arched recesses and there are short lengths of wall walk carried on arches on either side. Inside the gates are two single storey buildings facing each other, red brick with Portland stone dressings and hipped slate roofs. They have identical arcaded loggias on the front though their rears and interiors are very different. *AMS.*

Transverse Slipway and Gunboat Sheds, Haslar (1974)

GOSPORT

ROYAL NAVAL HOSPITAL, Haslar Road
MOD (Navy), Freehold

Instructions were issued in 1744 for the construction of naval hospitals at Plymouth, Portsmouth and Chatham to supersede the most unsatisfactory Contract System of care for sick and wounded seamen. The site at Haslar was purchased the following year after the conversion of Porchester Castle had been seriously considered. The hospital at Stonehouse was begun earlier but Haslar was in use first. *UCHB, Pevsner, A Revell; 'Haslar, The Royal Hospital,' Admiral P D G Pugh; 'The Planning of Haslar'; Journal of the RN Medical Service Vol 62.*

Main Block, Grade II*

The grandest of all Georgian naval buildings. Designed by the amateur architect Theodore Jacobsen, a merchant by trade but who had designed the Foundling Hospital in Bloomsbury then under construction. The plan took the form of double ranges linked at their centres and intersections around a square courtyard. The foundation stone was laid in 1746 and the main front block completed in 1754 though the first patients had been admitted the previous year. The side blocks were built between 1756 and 1762 though without their intended grand centre pieces. The quadrangle was never closed on its fourth side but a modern link block has unfortunately had to be constructed across the centre of the square.

The building is massively constructed in stock brick, of three storeys above a basement. The elevations are generally strictly functional, relieved only by a first floor level band course and parapet cornice. The main north east front has 43 bays and is 567' long. The double ranges are reflected in the doubled three bay terminal sections separated by a two window section. Only in the centrepiece are grand architectural gestures permitted.

The three bays centre piece is broken forward from the seven bay centre block and raised by a third floor. It has a Portland stone plinth and first and third floor level band courses and is crowned by a pediment containing splendid sculpture by Thomas Pierce with the Royal Arms and emblematic figures. The central archway has a toothed masonry surround linked by an impost band to the semicircular windows in arched recesses flanking it.

Royal Naval Hospital, Haslar

The first floor and arched second floor level windows are linked in stone surrounds with only a transom to separate them and the third floor windows also have plain surrounds. The side bays of the centre piece have supporting half-pediments at third floor level.

The centre of the ground floor has three parallel groin-vaulted aisles on stout arcades. In the paving of the centre aisle is preserved a section of the track way which originally ran down onto Haslar jetty to enable patients to be brought in from boats on trolleys. The rear of the range was originally an open arcade, now filled in.

The side ranges are similar to the front except that they have pedimented two storey centre pieces with single storey links to the ward blocks. There has been much alteration of fenestration, infilling of the areas between the double ranges and internal alteration. However the southern-most block retains its steeply pitched roof profile and internally its massive timber staircases with newel posts running the full height of the block.

Main Gate and Boundary Wall, Grade II

C1750. The hospital was sited in the north eastern half of a long rectangle enclosed by a high brick wall. Much of the wall survives though it is broken up by later buildings and openings. The Main Gate is axial with the Main Block in the centre of the north east side. The pair of plain wrought iron gates with a very elaborate overthrow are set between massive brick piers with Portland stone plinths and pedimented caps and were linked by iron railings on dwarf walls to pedestrian archways. The link on one side has been removed to facilitate traffic movement but should be reinstated when the new main entrance on the north west side is in service.

Residences 11,12 and 13,14, Grade II

Two pairs of houses facing each other across the main front of the hospital and built at the same time. Stock brick, three storeys, basement and attic. Three window front to each house with first floor and parapet level cornice, tiled mansard roofs. Enclosed wooden porches to the outer bays with iron area railings between. The south east pair has been extended to the southwest by two bays.

Main Gate, Royal Naval Hospital

Residences 13, 14, Royal Naval Hospital

GOSPORT   ROYAL NAVAL HOSPITAL

Laundry and Dispensary

Two relatively small buildings north west of the main block near the boundary wall, completed in 1762. They were the first deviation from the original proposals, confirming the abandoning of any intentions to build the fourth side of the main block. Plain rectangular two storey stock brick buildings with block entablatures and hipped roofs behind parapets. The Dispensary also has a first floor level block entablature and the centre three bays of the five window front are broken forward.

Dispensary, Royal Naval Hospital

1–5 Haslar Cottages, Grade II

Built into the eastern angle of the hospital grounds c1760. A two storey and attic stock brick terrace with cornice and parapet. The pairs are handed and there are blind recesses on the first floor over the doors.

1-5 Haslar Cottages, Royal Naval Hospital

St Luke's Chapel, Royal Naval Hospital

St Luke's Chapel, Grade II

A most charming building sited to the south west of the main block on its central axis. Completed in 1762. A simple rectangular red brick box with round-headed windows, pedimented gables and slate roof. The entrance front facing the main block has a pedimented Tuscan doorcase with a date plaque above and is surmounted by an octagonal timber bellcote with a weather vane. Flat roofed vestry extension at the rear. The interior was drastically renovated in 1963 and is immaculately maintained.

Gazebo

A late 18th C lookout sited south of the Main Block. A tall arcaded octagonal brick lower stage supports the open timber upper section with a concave pyramidal roof.

Haslar Terrace, Grade II

Management of the hospital was transferred from medical to executive command in 1795. The terrace, designed by the Architect to the Admiralty, Samuel Bunce, a pupil of James Wyatt, was built in 1796–98 to house the Governor and his staff.

The former Governor's house is in the centre of the group of three storeys and basement residences built of red brick with some burnt headers. It has first and second floor level band courses, a cornice and blocking course. The very tall first floor windows are set in square headed recesses. The enclosed porch and ground floor bay window have pilasters and entablatures. On either side are screen walls with gateways and lower set back links to the outer sections of the terrace. Each comprises three four window houses, with a cornice and blocking course and paved porches, timber on the left, brick on the right. The right hand section has been extended by a bay either end and each pair adapted to form three residences. The extreme left hand end house has received a mansard attic storey. In front are wrought iron area railings.

Haslar Terrace, Royal Naval Hsopital

Water Tower, Royal Naval Hospital

Water Tower, Grade II

1885, to the west of the main block, in the self confidently assertive style typical of the late 19th C naval buildings. A powerful square red brick tower with Portland stone dressings. Squat battered base with a simple arched entrance, separated by a roll moulding from the relatively tall shaft. On each face of this are two superimposed pairs of tall narrow windows, the upper ones with arched heads, in linked stone surrounds, a variation on the theme of the centrepiece of the Main Block. The tank occupies an attic stage between two deep bracketed cornices which has two oculi with keystoned surrounds on each face. The pyramidal roof rises in two stages. The interior is open to the underside of the massive tapered cast iron beams supporting the tank.

There were considerable additions to the hospital buildings between the turn of the century and the end of World War I to the west of the Main Block and either side of the Chapel and between the original grounds and the sea. The most important were the Pathology Laboratory, opened in 1899, Medical and Sisters' Messes, 1901, Zymotic Hospital, 1902, former Sick Officers' Block, 1905, former Psychiatric Block, 1910, and the Sick Berth Staff Quarters. All are substantial and generally attractive if not especially interesting buildings of red brick with stone dressings and pitched roofs. They appear in a particularly favourable light in comparison with the most recent additions to the Hospital.

GOSPORT

ROYAL NAVAL HOSPITAL

Fort Monkton, Military Road, Anglesey
MOD (Navy), Freehold
Ancient Monument, Grade II

1780–90. Brick and stone, an obtuse angled isosceles triangle on plan. The long base side is a casemated battery facing south east over the sea between demi-bastions, the north east one with a rounded salient. The two land fronts have a bastion at their junction and demi-bastions at the outer ends. The fort is enclosed by a dry moat with ravelins in front of the curtains. The junctions of the seaward and landward demi-bastions where normal flanking fire is not possible are protected by caponiers, a very advanced feature for the time. *AMS, Hogg, Williams.*

Fort Gilkicker, Military Road, Anglesey
MOD (Navy), Freehold
Grade II

1863–71. The 1859 Royal Commission recommended strengthening the battery built on Gilkicker point in 1796. In the event a new semi-circular 22 gun brick and granite casemated battery was built. The gorge is closed by a defensible barracks with a central entrance-way. The plans were amended during construction to provide iron shields for the casemates and five additional guns on the roof. The earth bank was thrown up around the battery when heavier guns were mounted on the roof c 1900. *AMS, Hogg, Williams.*

Fort Grange, HMS Sultan, Military Road, Brockhurst
Fort Rowner, HMS Centurion, Military Road, Brockhurst
MOD (Navy), Freehold
Ancient Monuments, Grade II

1853–63, with Fort Brockhurst, now in DOE Guardianship, filling the gap between Fort Gomer and Fort Elson to form a defensive line across the Gosport peninsula. Virtually identical brick and earth forts of an irregular hexagonal trace symmetrical about the central axis. The two faces to the field form a very obtuse angle with a massive caponier at the junctions, the flanks are angled slightly forward and covered by single sided caponiers. The gorge walls return nearly at right angles to the flanks to form an obtuse angle with the circular 'keep' at their intersection.

Casemated barracks occupy the rear of the ramparts and outer parts of the gorge walls. Two ramps at the angles of the face and flanks form traverses and access to the ramparts for ordnance. The flanks had casemated guns as well as those mounted on the rampart. The keep is built round a central courtyard and has its own small caponiers all round. It too was earth covered and adapted to mount artillery. The whole is surrounded by an immense ditch and the keep separated from the rest of the fort by a continuation of the ditch. The main entrance is in one side of the gorge adjacent to the keep and a second entrance on the axis of the keep and fort leads through the keep to the parade

Fort Rowner, Gosport

Fort Grange, Gosport

ground. The entrance arches are decorated in neo-Norman style.

The ditch at Fort Grange, which unlike the others was dry, has been partly filled in. It is probable that the forts were never armed as the threat which led to their construction had receded by the time they were completed. *AMS, UCHB, Balfour, Pevsner.*

Fort Elson, Military Road, Elson
MOD (Navy), Freehold
Ancient Monument

Construction was approved in 1852, along with the now dismantled Fort Gomer at the opposite, southern end of the line of forts across the Gosport peninsula. Built c 1855–60, but never armed. An irregular hexagonal brick and earth fort, considerably smaller and weaker than those in the centre of the line. The gorge is occupied by a single storey barracks block which while intended to be defensible would hardly have been capable of serious resistance. *AMS, Hogg.*

Fort Elson, Gosport

GOSPORT

ST GEORGE BARRACKS

ST GEORGE BARRACKS, Mumby Road
MOD (Army), Freehold

The barracks were built 1856–59 behind the late 18th C northern extension of the Gosport lines, on either side of the gateway. The possibility of their coming under bombardment was taken into account in the design although the Gomer – Elson line of forts was already under construction a mile and a half to the west. The flat roofs were given high parapets to retain an earth covering which was not in the event provided and the lower floor was half sunk into the ground to reduce the overall height. It is presumably this feature, together with the verandah to provide a covered assembly area on one of the blocks, which has inspired the myth that the design was intended for a tropical climate and sent to Hampshire in error. *Pevsner, Williams.*

Master Gunner's Quarters, St George Barracks

Master Gunner's Quarters, Grade II

Standing immediately inside the gateway in the Gosport lines and ante-dating the construction of the barracks. A late 18th C single storey five window block in red brick with burnt headers, extended two bays to the east in plain red brick in the first half of the 19th C, all under a hipped tiled roof. Now the Thrift Shop.

Gateway, Grade II

A tall single storey pale yellow brick block with a cornice and parapet. The boldly arcaded front has regrettably been painted. Surmounted by a large stone clock turret with Doric angle pilasters on a rusticated base, entablature and a pyramidal lead roof with a weather vane.

Gateway, St George Barracks, Gosport

GOSPORT

ST GEORGE BARRACKS

Blocks along Weevil Lane, St George Barracks, Gosport

Barrack Blocks along Weevil Lane, Grade II

Three long rectangular two storey blocks with their lower floors half sunk into the ground. Pale yellow brick with Portland stone upper floor level band courses, and cornices and parapets. The blocks are, from south to north, 24,18 and 18 bays long with gauged brick flat arches to sash windows and regularly arranged doorways on both floors. The doorways have plain surrounds with cornices and blocking courses; the upper ones are reached by flights of steps with elegant wrought iron handrails which are continued as railings along the top of the sunken area retaining walls. The blocks have received some alterations to their doorways and windows.

Block opposite the Gateway, Grade II

Just inside the southern half of the barracks across Mumby road from the gateway. In the same style as the barrack blocks but only three bays wide with a central doorway and four window flank walls.

Barrack Block along Clarence Road, Grade II

In the same style as the other barrack blocks but considerably longer and with a verandah along the eastern side of 57 cast iron columns resting on brick piers which form the lower colonnade.

Block along Clarence Road, St George Barracks, Gosport

Block opposite Gateway, St George Barracks

Lamp post in front of the Gateway, Grade II

A mid 19th C cast iron lamp post which formerly stood in Clarence Square. Above a wide plinth a classically moulded pedestal supports a spiral of dolphins around the hexagonal standard terminating in a relatively minute lamp.

Railings and Gates, Grade II

Both sections of the barracks are bounded by mid 19th C cast iron railings on a stone curb and there is a similar length on the other side of Weevil Lane now incorporated into Royal Clarence Yard. The gateways have open piers with the sides formed of a series of rings which are extended upwards as a tapering arched overthrow supporting a central lamp bracket. Similar but wider gateways without the arches mark the point where the royal railway line crossed Weevil Lane.

A section of track of the railway line cut through the Gosport lines in 1845 to allow Queen Victoria to travel directly to the jetty in Royal Clarence Yard en route to Osborne House is preserved behind the gateway.

Railings and Gates, St George Barracks

Lamp post, St George Barracks

GOSPORT

PRIDDY'S HARD
MOD (Navy), Freehold

Powder Magazine, Priddy's Hard, Gosport

Only a limited stock of gun powder was held at the Ordnance Wharf at Portsmouth. Most of the bulk was kept in the Square Tower at the seaward end of Portsmouth High Street which was most unsatisfactory in several respects. Priddy's Hard, the peninsula between Portsmouth Harbour and Forton Lake, had been fortified in the late 1750s to prevent it from being used by an enemy to bombard the harbour and dockyard and so was already Board of Ordnance land. Its remoteness from habitation made it an attractive location though only one of the three intended magazines was built to reduce the danger to shipping in the nearby deep water channel. Work began in 1769 under the direction of Captain John Archer and was largely completed by 1773. *AMS, Coad, Williams.*

Shifting House and Cooperage, Priddy's Hard

Fortifications

C 1757, moat and rampart with two demi-bastions and a sally port in the curtain, the moat now largely filled in.

Powder Magazine, Shifting House and Cooperage Ancient Monuments

C 1770, the original group out of which has grown the present extensive Royal Navy Armament Depot. The magazine is an immensely solid red brick block with two parallel barrel vaults divided by stout brick piers under a single pitched roof. It is massively buttressed on all four sides. Originally it was surrounded by a high brick wall which survives at either end.

The magazine is connected by a slightly later covered way to the centre of the range of buildings occupying the harbour side of its enclosure. This was originally two separate buildings used as the shifting house (changing room) and cooperage but they were linked together shortly after construction. Two storeys, brick with a first floor level band course on the original sections. The present slate roof has been raised several feet above the original corbelled eaves level.

These buildings now house an excellent museum of naval armaments, accessible by appointment.

Offices, Priddy's Hard, Gosport

Comber Basin, Priddy's Hard, Gosport

Camber Basin, Ancient Monument

It was originally intended to build a timber rolling way for the powder barrels across the 200 yards of mud flats to the deep water channel. Instead an attractive small octagonal stone basin was constructed, linked to the magazine by a covered way, with a dredged channel for lighters.

Offices south east of the Powder Magazine

Late 18th C, not to be identified with the now vanished Storekeeper's House of 1777 which lay further to the south. Two storeys, red brick with burnt headers, cornice and parapet. Seven bay front, the centre three broken forward and pedimented, with a clock face in the tympanum. Gauged brick arches to sash windows. Doorway with large semi-circular fanlight and side-lights.

Workshops, Ancient Monuments

Three small rectangular single storey slate roofed red brick buildings between the Powder Magazine and the Camber. The northern one is mid 19th C but the other two which form part of the museum are relatively modern.

Victorian Magazine

1878, built into the north demi-bastion. Brick with twin barrel-vaulted chambers. Two rare timber over-head travelling cranes survive inside.

GOSPORT

ROYAL CLARENCE VICTUALLING YARD,
Weevil Lane
MOD (Navy), Freehold

Provisioning of the fleet was the responsibility of the Victualling Board, which was abolished as a separate department in 1832. Before the creation of a unified yard in the late 1820's facilities were scattered on both sides of the harbour. By the early 18th C there was a large brewery with its cooperage at what was then called Weevil Yard. As all bulk storage of food and drink was then in casks the cooperage was a central part of victualling operations. In 1766 it was decided to concentrate all cooperage at Weevil Yard and a new cooperage was built there which remained in use until the abolition of the naval rum issue in 1970.

With the experience of coping with the demands of the Napoleonic wars the Board determined in 1815 to completely rebuild its establishments at both Portsmouth and Plymouth. Stonehouse was given priority and not until 1828 did work begin at Gosport where it had been decided to centralise operations. All the buildings on the site were demolished except the cooperage and additional land acquired from the Board of Ordnance. Rebuilding was virtually complete by 1832. In 1831 the yard was renamed after the Lord High Admiral, the Duke of Clarence.

The buildings designed by G L Taylor, Civil Architect to the Navy Board, were distinguished if not so monumental as Rennie's at Plymouth. Most of the foodstuffs arrived and left by water, except for the meat which came on the hoof, until the coming of the railway. The yard suffered severely from bombing in the last war and is now used for storage of mainly non-food stuffs. *AMS, UCHB, Coad.*

Cooperage Green, Royal Clarence Yard

Cooperage Green, Ancient Monuments

Late 1760s, four ranges of heterogeneous single storey pitched roofed buildings around a roughly rectangular court. Some are brick, others are timber framed, with a mixture of tile, asbestos and corrugated iron roofs. Some of the buildings have been bombed and rebuilt. In the middle of the west side of the green is an octagonal single storey brick pump house with a timber louvre on top of the tiled roof. The buildings ceased to be a cooperage with the withdrawal of the naval rum issue in 1970.

Mill, Granary and Bakery, Ancient Monument

C 1830, the principal structure of Taylor's rebuilding of the Yard. The granary is brought forward to the quayside to permit direct unloading from vessels and raised on an open ground storey of massive cast iron columns to avoid blocking the wharf. The three upper storeys have a conventional Georgian exterior of red brick with stone band courses and cornices and a dormered attic in the hipped slate roof. The internal structure is more innovative with cast iron columns supporting the massive timber floors needed to carry the grear weight of the grain.

The three storey bakery wing is set back from the water's edge on the north side of the granary, the corresponding store wing on the south side having been destroyed by bombing. It is similar in character to the granary, though with relatively little use of cast iron members. The pedimented centre piece and terminal feature have solid arches extending from the ground into the first floor. The bank of nine ovens for ships' biscuit survive, disused, at the back of the ground floor, with the walled coal yard behind. The building was operated with steam driven machinery designed by the younger Rennie.

Granery, Royal Clarence Yard

GOSPORT   ROYAL CLARENCE VICTUALLING YARD

Mill, Granery and Bakery, Royal Clarence Yard

Main Gate and Residences, Royal Clarence Yard

GOSPORT

ROYAL CLARENCE VICTUALLING YARD

Main Gate and Residences, Ancient Monument, Grade II

C 1830, making a splendid formal entrance to the yard. The tall central archway has a fine pair of iron gates. It is flanked by paired Doric pilasters with entablature and blocking course surmounted by two royal coats of arms. On either side are square-headed pedestrian entrances. The flanking screen walls are blank on the outside but fronted with elegant curving Doric colonnades on the inside which are linked to the residences at their extremities.

The houses of the Superintendent and his deputy form the north side of the square inside the main gate. Each is of two storeys, basement and attic, painted stucco with a four window front with a plain entablature and blocking course in front of the hipped slate roof. Facing them across the square and striving manfully to maintain the symmetry is the much smaller Porter's Lodge, with a three window front and only one room deep.

Slaughterhouse, Ancient Monument

Early 19th C. A tall single storey rectangular red brick block, twelve bays long, with stone plinth and impost band to the arcaded side walls with round-headed sash windows. A row of ventilators is set under the eaves of the hipped slate roof which has a central monitor with louvred sides, now sheeted in.

Royal Railway Station, Ancient Monument

Gosport Station had been constructed outside the Gosport lines in 1841 because the Board of Ordnance refused to countenance an opening through. In 1845 they were obliged to concede a single track line through to the royal jetty from which Queen Victoria embarked for Osborne. One wall of the original royal railway shelter remains embedded in later extensions and converted to a store. Red brick with arched sash windows, all severely eroded by salt decay.

Slaughter house, Royal Clarence Yard

LYMINGTON

55 High Street
Government Offices, Freehold
Grade II, Group Value, Conservation Area

A three storey 18th C house with a painted brick four window front. Sash windows with glazing bars, those on the first floor being replacements. The ground floor now has a reproduction Georgian bow and a modern door. Modillion eaves cornice and hipped tiled roof. *UCHB*

PORTSMOUTH

A Note on the Portsmouth Harbour Defences

Portsmouth is the best place in the country to study on the ground the whole development of artillery fortifications. Much remains especially of the later phases and the vanished portions are well documented. A considerable part of the surviving defences are still in MOD occupation and to appreciate their significance it is necessary to place them in the context of the history of fortification in general and the Portsmouth Harbour defences in particular.

The history of the defence of Portsmouth Harbour begins with the building of the Roman Saxon Shore fort at Porchester Castle in the 3rd C, later to become a major medieval royal fortress. Portsmouth itself was only of minor importance during the early medieval period; until the 15th C the defences were entirely of earth and timber. The building of Southsea Castle by Henry VIII in 1538–40 signalled the real beginning of the artillery revolution at Portsmouth. In the second half of the 16th C the town became the only one in the country apart from Berwick-on-Tweed to receive fortifications on the latest Italian model with angled bastions.

The Restoration ushered in a new era of building and from 1665 onwards under the direction of Sir Bernard de Gomme the Portsmouth fortifications were radically reconstructed and Gosport fortified with a massive bastioned line. The Dockyard, which was distinct from the town, was defended by a simple earth rampart, replaced in 1704 by a brick wall for security rather than defence. Improvements continued throughout the first half of the 18th C culminating in the establishment of Fort Cumberland at Eastney in 1745. In the 1770s the Dockyard and its growing dependent town of Portsea were enclosed by fortifications linked to those of Portsmouth proper. The Gosport defences were elaborated and extended to include the then Weevil Yard and Priddy's Hard. The Napoleonic period saw the modernisation of existing works and construction of new, particularly Fort Monkton near Gilkicker Point.

The growing power of artillery pushed defences out from the object to be protected. In the 1850s Hilsea Lines were built along the narrow Port Creek, which separates Portsea island from the mainland, and Stokes Bay Lines were built SW of Gosport. A line of forts was also begun to isolate the Gosport peninsula. Public alarm at the development of the French ironclad navy drove Lord Palmerston to appoint a Royal Commission to Consider the Defences of the United Kingdom in 1859 and to implement its recommendations, albeit in reduced form.

The Royal Commission's report of 1860 covered all the defended areas from the Thames to Milford Haven. For the Portsmouth area it proposed dramatic new works in addition to modernisation of existing ones. The most original were the great circular sea forts planted on shoals in the Solent to resist naval attack, a unique group though individual examples were built at Portland, Plymouth and Bermuda. Against attack from a force which had made a landing elsewhere a line of forts was proposed running west from Langstone Harbour along the Portsdown ridge, turning south around the head of Fareham Lake and crossing the Gosport peninsula to meet the sea again at Lee on Solent. In the event the Gosport forts already under construction were deemed adequate and only the northern fort of the second Gosport line at Fareham was built to link them to the Portsdown forts. None the less this made Portsmouth the only British city with defences comparable to contemporary continental examples such as Paris and Vienna.

The Gymnasium, Burnaby Road
MOD (Navy), Freehold
Grade II

Mid 19th C, built as a drill hall or riding school. Large yellow brick block with rusticated angle piers, plinth and brick dentil cornice. Arcaded flanks with semi-circular headed windows. The gables are treated as open pediments. Lower projections at either end. The building has been burnt out and it is proposed to convert it to squash courts.*UCHB.*

King James Gate, Burnaby Road
MOD (Navy) Freehold
Ancient Monument

1687, built to provide access to the Point when this was cut off from Old Portsmouth by the extension of the defences between the town and the Camber. It has been moved twice since the defences were dismantled and reduced to a facade shorn of its pediment and turret. A rusticated Portland stone vehicular archway enclosed by coupled Corinthian pilasters and entablature and flanked by smaller pedestrian archways. *AMS, Pevsner.*

PORTSMOUTH

King James Gate, Portsmouth

Mill Dam House, Burnaby Road
MOD (Navy), Freehold
Grade II, Conservation Area

C1840, the only part of the former Mill Dam Barracks still occupied by MOD. Square two storey block with seven window elevations, the centre three bays broken forward and pedimented. Red brick with burnt headers, Portland stone plinths and first floor level band course to centrepieces, brick cornice with rendered blocking course. Pedimented centres, hipped slate roof. *UCHB.*

Mill Dam House, Portsmouth

Careers Information Office, Cambridge Road
MOD (Army), Freehold

Dated 1908, a former schoolhouse. A single storey red brick block with terracotta dressings. Flemish style gables to the slate roof, date plaque in the main one. A free standing display kiosk has been constructed in form of the building which although partly obscuring it has avoided the need to form a display window in it.

144

PORTSMOUTH

**ROYAL MARINE BARRACKS, Cromwell Road,
Eastney**
MOD (Navy), Freehold
Conservation Area (except St Andrew's Church)

Built to house the Royal Marine Artillery. Splendidly sited with its tree lined parade ground looking across the Solent, the barracks is at one end of the conservation area which stretches uninterrupted along the sea front past Southsea Castle as far as Porstmouth Point. *AMS, UCHB, Hogg, Balfour.*

Eastney Batteries, Ancient Monument, Grade II

The batteries ante-date the barracks. The east and west batteries together with the now virtually disappeared Lumps Fort to the west were built in the Napoleonic period to fill the gap between Fort Cumberland and Southsea Castle. They were undergoing reconstruction at the time of the 1859 Royal Commission. The open batteries were linked by a covered way and were never fully armed. Much of the ditches and covered way has been levelled.

Main Gate and Boundary Wall
Ancient Monument, West side Grade II

1862–67, 12′ high flint wall with brick dressings matching the battery walls, the upper part pierced with regular close set firing loops, surrounding the trapezium of the original barrack area. The north side, now much demolished, took the form of curtains either side of a central bastion with demibastions at each end. The east side was broken through when the barracks area was enlarged. The south side returns at each end only as far as the outer angles of the Eastney Batteries, the intervening gap having been filled by the covered way linking the batteries.

The Main Gate is in the middle of the west side. Originally it had two vehicular passages flanked by pedestrian arches with piers between but the central pier has been removed. Built of banded rusticated brickwork with stone copings and pedimented capstones with iron lamp standards. Mortars are set over the pedestrian archways.

Officers' Mess, Grade II

1862–70 on the east side of the long rectangular parade ground. Three storeys, basement and attic. The seven bay centre is stone faced with the main wall recessed behind a two storey loggia. The ground floor of the loggia is plain with segmental arches. The first floor is arcaded between Tuscan pilasters, coupled in the slightly projecting central bay. The main entrance is at this level approached by a monumental divided stairway. The stair balustrade is continued along the arcade and repeated as the second floor balcony front and as the main parapet. The second floor has round headed windows and the centre is crowned with an elaborate Royal Arms flanked by the royal monogram.

The wings are red brick with yellow brick quoins and frieze and a stone plinth offset, first floor sill level band course and eaves cornice, slate mansard roof and dormers. Each wing has eight bays, the three nearest the centre broken forward with the central bay picked out with rusticated yellow brick work and a pedimented stone attic dormer. The interior has a ground staircase and a superb dining room with a central semi-circular bay, upper gallery and massive coved ceiling which is now the Royal Marines' Museum.

Officers' Mess, Royal Marine Barracks

PORTSMOUTH   ROYAL MARINE BARRACKS

Eastney Terrace, Royal Marine Barracks

Officers' Mess, Royal Marine Barracks

Long Barracks

1860s, an essential element of the group forming as it does the north side of the parade ground. A three storey 77 window block over 1000′ long made up of seven sets of barrack rooms flanking projecting three bay staircase blocks. It has far less architectural pretensions than the officers' buildings. Red brick with stone band courses at first and second floor sill levels, hipped slate roofs. Linked by triple archways surmounted by mortars to the buildings at either end.

Eastney Terrace, Grade II

1862–70, at the west end of the parade ground, two blocks at right angles forming a balanced but not rigidly symmetrical composition viewed from the foreshore. At the west end is the four bay Eastney House, deeper than the row of six officers' houses of three windows each to which it is joined. These are linked by a triple archway to the four bay south end of the CO's house which with the HQ offices makes a ten window front towards the parade ground. The blocks are similar in detail to the wings of the Officers' Mess, three storeys attic and basement, rusticated yellow brick quoins and dividing strips and frieze; stone plinth offset, first floor sill level band course, eaves and gable pediment cornices. The windows are semi-circular headed on the ground floor and segmented above, with stone surrounds on the south and west elevations. Slate roofs with dormers.

Old Barracks Offices

1860s, balancing the east block of Eastney Terrace on the west side of the parade ground, though less elaborate architecturally. Three storey red brick block with rusticated angles and pedimented gables. Fronted by a ten bay single storey arcaded covered way. Slate roofed.

PORTSMOUTH

ROYAL MARINE BARRACKS

Long Barracks, Royal Marine Barracks

Clock Tower/Water Tower, Grade II

1870–71, an extraordinary four square six storey red brick tower in Vanbrughesque style. The lower three storeys have two semi-circular headed windows in each side, stone string courses at first and third floor level. The third floor has three pairs of semi-circular windows on each face and the fourth five oculi in a sunken rectangular panel. The walls are battered up to the stone mock machicolations at sixth floor level which has a clock face in the centre of each side flanked by blind oculi. The slate roof is a truncated pyramid with a pedimented dormer in each side and an elaborate iron railing around the flagstaff on the top. A circular stair turret is corbelled out from the north-east angle with a conical roof crowned by a weather vane. The other corners have paired chimneys linked by arches set across them.

Clock/Water Tower, Royal Marine Barracks

St Andrew's Church

1905, a sturdy Admiralty pattern early English style church similar to those at RM Deal and the RN barracks at Chatham and Devonport. Broad basilican nave with an apsidal baptistry at the west end and porches at the west ends of the aisles. Aisleless chancel, square ended in this case, flanked by vestries on the north side and the organ loft over the porch on the south. Red brick with Portland stone dressings, Westmorland slate roofs. Grouped lancet windows, wall arcading internally. Open timber trussed roof to nave and aisles, barrel ceiling to the chancel.

St Andrew's Church, Royal Marine Barracks

PORTSMOUTH

HM NAVAL BASE, The Hard
MOD (Navy), Freehold

The following extremely brief summary of the history of the dockyard and description of its historic buildings in no way does justice to their importance and interest.

The present dockyard was founded by Henry VII in 1495 on eight acres of land half a mile north of the medieval centre of Portsmouth. He commissioned the building of a dry dock near the present No 1 Basin. Major development and expansion took place in the second half of the 17th C, new docks were built and the yard fortified. By the 1720s Portsmouth was the country's major dockyard.

During the 18th C the dockyard was progressively enlarged northwards into the harbour and southwards towards the town. Brick became the usual material for the construction of numerous new buildings and replacements for timber structures decayed with age or destroyed by fire.

The Napoleonic period saw revolutionary developments of world wide importance under the Inspector Generalship of Sir Samuel Bentham. The Great (now No 1) Basin was rebuilt with the first use in England of the caisson gate. He pioneered fire proof buildings and adequate provision for fire-fighting and installed the first steam power in any dockyard at Porstmouth. He also sponsored Brunel in the establishment of the Block Mills.

After the post-Napoleonic hiatus expansion of the dockyard began again in 1843 with the construction of the Steam (now No 2) Basin. The last major expansion which began in 1867 nearly trebled the area of the dockyard with the construction of three new basins, amalgamated to form the present No 3 Basin in 1912. The dockyard buildings suffered heavily from bombing in the last war.

The pre-Victorian buildings in the naval base are confined to the area south of No 2 Basin which is designated as a Conservation Area. Most pre-Victorian buildings are scheduled as Ancient Monuments and some of the Victorian ones. The buildings are described so far as possible in chronological order, earlier names are given in brackets. *AMS, Balfour, Coad, Pevsner.*

No 1 Basin and Docks 1–6
Ancient Monument, Conservation Area

C1690 et seq.. The Great Ship Basin was originally built in 1691–98 together with the Great Stone Dock (5), a building slip on the site of Dock 3 and a smaller basin to the north. In 1700 Dock 6 was formed in the entrance to the North Basin, which in 1772 was made into the Reservoir. Dock 4 was built on the site of a building slip of 1754 in the same year. During 1795–1801 No 1 Basin was enlarged by 50% and fitted with a caisson gate, since renewed. Dock 1 was built in 1801, 2 in 1802 and 3 in 1803. HMS Victory was permanently berthed in Dock 2 in 1922. The Mary Rose has been brought to Dock 3.

No 1 Basin and Docks 1-5, HM Naval Base, Portsmouth

PORTSMOUTH   HM NAVAL BASE

HISTORIC AREA HM NAVAL BASE PORTSMOUTH

1	No 1 Basin and Docks 1-6	15	St Anne's Church
2	Main Gate	16	South Office Block
3	Dockyard Wall	17	Short Row
4	Police Office	18	North Office Block
5	1-9 The Parade	19	RN Film Corporation
6	Statue of William III	20	Block Mills
7	Staff Officers' Mess	21	Ship Maintenance Authority Office
8	9, 10, 11 Stores	22	Fire Station
9	No 18 Store (Great Ropehouse)	23	No 6 Boathouse
10	Boiler Shop West	24	Iron and Brass Foundry
11	No 19 Store	25	5, 7 Boathouses
12	15, 16, 17 Stores	26	Royal Railway Shelter
13	24, 25 Stores and YSM's Office	27	Captain Scott Memorial
14	Admiralty House	28	Semaphore Tower and Lion Gate

PORTSMOUTH

Main Gate and Dockyard Wall
Ancient Monument, Conservation Area

1704-11 on the line of earth fortifications built under Sir Bernard de Gomme in 1666–67. The gate was widened by 10′ in 1942–43 and the overthrow lost.

Police Office (Porters' Lodge)
Ancient Monument, Conservation Area

1708. The porters were in charge of the watchmen and their lodge is still the control centre for dockyard security. A two storey five window Georgian brick house, now rendered and painted, with cornice, parapet and a slate roof.

1–9 The Parade (Long Row or the Terrace)
Ancient Monument, Conservation Area

1717 as Principal Officers' Lodgings. An originally symmetrical terrace of nine red brick houses, Nos 1, 5 and 9 broken slightly forward; three storeys and basement with panelled parapet, each front five

Main Gate and Police Office

windows. The front and ends of the terrace have been rendered and painted and enclosed porches added in the early 19th C. The glazing bars are partly intact.

No 9 at the south end, was greatly enlarged in 1832 to make the Admiral Superintendent's House (Spithead House) with the end becoming an elaborate main elevation fronting onto its own drive. It has a grand porch with coupled Doric columns and an iron and glass canopy. The mound in the garden covers an ice house of c 1840.

1-9 The Parade, HM Naval Base, Portsmouth

No 9, The Parade, HM Naval Base

Statue of William III, Conservation Area

Presented by Col Richard Norton in 1717 and originally set up in front of Long Row, later moved to in front of Admiralty House. Gilt bronze standing figure in Roman imperial armour on Portland stone pedestal.

Staff Officers' Mess (RN Academy)
Ancient Monument, Conservation Area

1729–32 as Royal Naval Academy. Three storeys and basement, red brick with Portland stone quoins, band courses, cornice and coping. Nine bay front with slightly projecting three bay centre with pedimented stone Doric doorcase. Strongly projecting pedimented wings housed the Professor and Captain Superintendent.

The Academy closed in 1806 and it was remodelled for the Royal Naval College, which opened in 1808, with the addition of the timber and lead central cupola crowned by a golden orb. The College removed to Greenwich in 1875. It became the School of Navigation (HMS Dryad) in 1906, which transferred to Southwik House after bomb damage in 1941. *see Front Cover.*

King William III, HM Naval Base

9, 10, 11 Stores, HM Naval Base

9, 10, 11 Stores, Ancient Monuments, Conservation Area

1763, North, 1776, Middle and 1782, South Present Use Stores. A symmetrical group of three storey thirteen bay blocks with projecting pedimented three bay centrepieces. Red brick with Portland stone dressings, hipped slate faced mansard roofs. The centre of No 10 which terminates the vista down Anchor Lane has a rusticated stone archway through it and had a fine clock tower and cupola until blitzed in 1941. The north half of the roof was burnt at the same time and rebuilt with a gabled mansard with steep tiled faces.

No 11 at the north end was partly burnt out in 1874 but rebuilt and now has the best preserved interior. All three have unsightly lift motor houses on the roof. In 1972–3 the ground floors of all buildings were converted to museum and visitors' uses and arcades opened in the front of Nos 9 and 10. The upper floors were evacuated in 1976 because of structural and fire precaution problems.

9, 10 Stores, HM Naval Base, Portsmouth

No 18 Store (Great Ropehouse), Ancient Monument, Conservation Area

1770, a three storey brick double ropehouse 1095' long. Replaced one of 1760 destroyed by fire which had replaced two timber ropehouses, also burnt, on the site of the original ropehouse of 1665. Burnt in its turn by Jack the Painter in 1776 but rebuilt. Until the middle of this century it was virtually unaltered except for the cutting through of archways on the line of College Road.

In 1954–61 it was disembowelled, the upper floors removed and the roof replaced with a flat-topped mansard with tiled faces on single span steel trusses and projecting eaves. The windows, gutters and down pipes were callously replaced. Three storey high steel folding doors were hacked in the ends and five pairs of two storey doors in the flanks.

No 18 Store, HM Naval Base, Portsmouth

Boiler Shop West, HM Naval Base, Portsmouth

No 19 Store, HM Naval Base, Portsmouth

Boiler Shop West, Ancient Monument, Conservation Area

1770, as the Hemp Tarring House. A two storey red brick block, much altered.

15, 16, 17 Stores, Ancient Monuments, Conservation Area

1771, East Sea Store (No 15), West Hemp House (No 16) and 1778, East Hemp Store (No 17). A line of three storey red brick blocks of similar form with buttressed flanks. The east end of No 16 has a flag, crown, GRYIII and 1771 picked out in grey bricks and No 17 has 1771 at the east end.

There was a fourth Store, No 14, to the west until it was bombed; No 16 was reduced to a shell and the other two damaged by bombing. All three have been modernised with concrete and steel columns and floors, metal windows and large steel folding doors inserted. The roofs have been rebuilt as flat topped mansards with tiled faces and projecting eaves.

No 19 Store, Ancient Monument, Conservation Area

1771, as the Hatchelling House and Hemp House, linked to the Ropery by a covered way carried across Stony Lane on arches. The courtyard between the two buildings was roofed over early in this century.

**25 and 25, Stores and Yard Services Manager's Offices
Ancient Monuments, Conservation Area**

1782–83, forming with Store 34 of 1708, destroyed in the last war, the north and south sides of the former Parade Ground, now built over. Rectangular blocks each with a central courtyard. Originally two storeys with Portland stone first floor band courses, brick dentil cornices to parapet walls, pediments over centre and ends on Parade elevations. No 24 and the YSM's Offices have been raised a storey.

No 16 Store, HM Naval Base, Portsmouth

Yard Services Manager's Offices

Admiralty House, HM Naval Base, Portsmouth

Admiralty House, Ancient Monument, Conservation Area

1784–86 by Samuel Wyatt, Thomas Telford possibly being Clerk of Works. Yellow brick with Portland stone dressings. Five window central block, three storeys and basement, with plinth, ground and first floor sill level band courses, dentil eaves cornice and blocking course, hipped slate roof. Three window single storey links with balustraded parapets. Tall single storey wings of one wide pedimented bay. Gauged brick cambered arches to sash windows with glazing bars.

The delicate octagonal lantern on a square base is not part of Wyatt's original design. The proportions of the front are wrecked by external shutters on the first and second floors. The original delicate Doric porch has been replaced by a clumsy block with an iron and glass canopy. The sides and rear are much encumbered with additions and excrescences and draped with plumbing. The fine interiors were damaged by bombing.

St Anne's Dockyard Church, Conservation Area

St Anne's Dockyard Church, Portsmouth

1785–87 by John Marquand, to replace the original chapel of 1704 whose site was required for Admiralty House. A typical red brick Georgian preaching box. Wide rectangular nave with small projecting chancel. Two storey elevations to allow galleries around most of three sides, semi-circular heads to upper windows, segmental to lower. The west end was bombed in 1940 and shortened by a bay when rebuilt in 1955–6, with a reconstruction of the original cupola over the pedimented gable. The interior was most satisfactorily restored and fortunately the large ceiling rose was preserved in situ.

South Office Block, HM Naval Base, Portsmouth

South Office Block, Ancient Monument, Conservation Area

The western part 1786 as offices, the eastern 1788 as a storehouse. A pair of two storey pedimented brick blocks with Portland stone dressings. Linked in 1840 by a three storey central block with triple archway in rusticated stone ground floor. Two painted timber porches on the western block.

Short Row, Ancient Monument, Conservation Area.

1787, supervised by Thomas Telford. A five house red brick terrace, three storeys and basement, cornice and parapet, Portland stone first floor band course. Four window fronts except No 10 at the north end which is two windows. No 14 has single storey addition on its south side. Painted timber porches, cast iron area railings. The houses and gardens occupy the site of a bastion of the 17th C fortifications.

Short Row, HM Naval Base, Portsmouth

North Office Block (The Smithery)
Ancient Monument, Conservation Area

1791, a rectangular two storey red brick block.

RN Film Corporation (Pay Office), Conservation Area

1798, an early example of fire-proof construction, with brick cross-vaulting on cast iron springings and columns. The first floor was destroyed in the blitz.

    The round arched exterior is concealed by verandahs which have been enclosed later.

North Office Block, HM Naval Base

Block Mills, Ancient Monument, Conservation Area

C 1800 by Sir Samuel Bentham, over the top of the 1690s North Basin which was levelled up by the insertion of two storeys of brick vaulting, the upper intended for storage, the lower continuing as a reservoir for the dockyard pumping station. Two parallel three storey brick blocks, with a single storey link built later to house the revolutionary block making machinery of Marc Isambard Brunel, which still exists though no longer in situ. Due to be taken into DAMHB Guardianship.

Ship Maintenance Authority Office

Ship Maintenance Authority Office
Ancient Monument, Conservation Area

1815–17, by Edward Holl, opened as School of Naval Architecture, later Technical School, Tactical School and Central Communications Office. Two storeys and basement, yellow stock brick with Portland stone dressings. Seventeen bay front to Admiralty Green, three bay pedimented centre piece and two bay ends broken forward boldly with arcaded ground floor. Stone plinth, impost string, first floor band course, cornice and blocking course. Boldly projecting Doric porch, gauged brick camber arches to sash windows. Cast iron area railings.

Fire Station, Ancient Monument, Conservation Area

1843–45 to replace the timber tank serving the salt water ring main installed by General Bentham in 1800. Two tiers of cast iron columns with semiclassical capitals linked by girders with elliptical lower chords and open spandrels. The tank they supported was removed in 1950. The space under the tank was originally left open for timber stacking but later enclosed with corrugated iron sheet.

Fire Station, HM Naval Base, Portsmouth

No 6 Boathouse, HM Naval Base, Portsmouth

No 6 Boathouse, Ancient Monument, Conservation Area

1845, built as a mast house on the side of the old mast pond of 1665 to which it is linked by a slipway. Three storey yellow brick block with Portland stone plinth, first floor band course, cornice and blocking course. Three large archways with stone impost blocks and keystones give onto the mast point. The south east corner is splayed off to accommodate College Road.

The chief interest of the building is the interior which is a magnificent example of early Victorian cast iron construction designed to carry immense loads. The columns support massive beams trussed with wrought iron tie bars and the timber floor boards rest on cast iron joists. Additional columns support the framing around access openings in the floor.

The east end suffered severe bomb damage in 1941 and has been curtailed on the upper floors though the external walls are intact up to second floor level.

No 2 Ship Shop, HM Naval Base, Portsmouth

PORTSMOUTH   HM NAVAL BASE

No 2 Ship Shop, Ancient Monument

1849, along narrow red brick block with Portland stone dressings stretching the length of the west side of the former Steam Basin (No 2). Of Vanbrugh-like scale and appearance. Two arcaded storeys, the tall lower one intended for the assembly of reciprocating steam engines and the low upper one as a sail loft.

Iron and Brass Foundry, Ancient Monument, Conservation Area

1854, similar in scale and style to No 2 Ship Shop. A variously two and three storey L-shaped red brick block with Portland stone dressings. Segmental-headed ground floor windows, round-headed windows in the upper storeys.

Holy Trinity Church Ruins

1841, by Augustus Livesay, built to serve the norther part of Portsea but absorbed by the Dockyard Extension and became for a time the RN Church. Bombed in the last war and now a landscaped ruin.

Iron and Brass Foundry, HM Naval Base

Unicorn Gate, HM Naval Base, Portsmouth

Dockyard Extension Wall and Unicorn Gate Ancient Monuments

1867 Portland stone rubble wall with brick coursing and stitching; sentry 'pulpits' corbelled out at intervals. Unicorn Gate was originally built in 1779 as the north gate of Portsea but was moved in 1868 to form the entrance to the Dockland Extension. Rusticated Portland stone archway between coupled Doric pilasters supporting an entablature and pediment, with a sculptured unicorn in the tympanum, flanked by pedestrian archways in upswept screen walls. The gateway now sits forlornly in the middle of a roundabout and has been stripped of its gates which have been set up meaninglessly in front of the former Dockyard Apprentices' School.

Round Tower

Re-erected in 1853, having been originally built in 1683 on the harbour shore north of old Portsmouth and east of the then dockyard. Now rather neo-Norman in appearance, little if any of the original work survives. Three storeys in Portland stone, the lowest battered with an arched corbel table string course, and crowned with a false-machicolated parapet. Tall thin rectangular windows in each storey. Not to be confused with the Round Tower near the Point.

Round Tower, HM Naval Base, Portsmouth

PORTSMOUTH   HM NAVAL BASE

Frederick's Battery

Originally built alongside the Round Tower in 1688 and also re-erected in a modified form nearby in the mid 19th C. Its present configuration is a row of six masonry casemates surmounted by a rampart walk with a tower at each end.

Frederick Battery, HM Naval Base

5 and 7 Boathouses, Ancient Monuments, Conservation Area

1875 (No 7) and 1882 (No 5) built as mast houses, on cast iron stilts over part of the old mast pond. Single storey weather boarded timber framed sheds with small paned sash windows, reminiscent of the vanished timber dockyard buildings of the first half of the 18th C. No. 5 Boathouse is being converted into a museum by the Mary Rose Trust.

No 7 Boathouse, HM Naval Base, Portsmouth

No 1 Pumping Station

1878, two storeys, brick with stone dressings, strangely mannered external detailing, arcaded ground floor. Circular upper windows set in recessed panels. Tall brick chimney with dentil cornice. Elegant cast iron interior structure.

Royal Railway Shelter, HM Naval Base

Gunnery Equipment Store

1892, in similar style to No 1 Pumping Station.

Royal Railway Shelter, South Railway Jetty Ancient Monument, Conservation Area

1893, for use en route to Osborne House, a slender open sided canopy with a cast iron frame.

Paint Shop

1896, a single storey red brick block with Portland stone dressings and rusticated brick quoins. Tall arcaded windows with an impost band, plain entablature with moulded cornice and parapet, pedimented gables.

Captain Scott Memorial, Conservation Area

A bronze standing figure by his widow Lady Kathleen Scott, on a massive granite pedestal.

Captain Scott Memorial, HM Naval Base

PORTSMOUTH   HM NAVAL BASE

Semaphore Tower and Lion Gate
Ancient Monument (Gate only), Conservation Area

1926–29, a neo-Georgian rebuilding of structures destroyed by fire in 1913. The five storey red brick tower with Portland stone string courses and entablature is crowned with a stone reconstruction of the early 18th C terminus of the London-Portsmouth semaphore line, a tall octagonal Ionic pavilion capped by a small lookout and a mast. The most eye-catching building in the dockyard as seen from the Gosport ferry.

The ground stage incorporates on its west side the former Lion Gate of Portsea, originally built in 1778, dismantled in 1871, also called the Gate way of Empire. A rusticated Portland stone archway between coupled Doric attached columns with vermiculated alternate drums supporting an entablature and pediment with a sculptured lion in pediment, flanked by pedestrian arches.

St Agatha's Church, Grade II*

1893–95 by J H Ball, pupil of Waterhouse, for Father R R Rolling, an evangelistic Anglo-Catholic, on a site them hemmed in by one of the worst slums in Portsmouth. A brick Early Christian style basilica, the intended north aisle and western narthex were never built. The tower at the west end of the south aisle was truncated just above nave roof level. The short four bay nave is very broad with massive timber trusses. In 1901 Heywood Sumner, a disciple of William Morris, began the decoration of the east wall, apse and semi-dome with magnificent sgraffito work.

It ceased to be a church in 1955 and became a naval store, the surrounding housing having been destroyed by bombing and clearance so that it stands gauntly exposed to view in a way that was never anticipated. The fittings were dispersed and intermediate floors inserted. The Lady Chapel at the east end of the south aisle, also with sgraffito decoration by Heywood Sumner, was destroyed for road construction in 1964 and the remainder of the church is now similarly threatened.

Fort Southwick, Portsmouth

Fort Southwick, Military Road, Portsdown
MOD (Navy), Freehold
Ancient Monument, Grade II

1861–70, the centre of the line of forts along Portsdown ridge recommended by the 1859 Royal Commission. A large brick and stone fort of irregular though symmetrical shape surrounded by a dry ditch. Massive double caponier at the angle between

the fort faces and single caponiers masking the flanks. The defensible barracks in the centre of the gorge is separated from the body of the fort by its own dry ditch; its outer face has two demi-bastions at the extremities and a neo-Norman entranceway in the centre. The fort never received any armament though it was for many years the HQ of the Royal Garrison Artillery. *AMS, UCHB, Hogg.*

PORTSMOUTH

HMS NELSON ROYAL NAVAL BARRACKS,
Queen Street
MOD (Navy), Freehold
Conservation Area

When the Admiralty finally decided to construct a Naval Barracks at Portsmouth they purchased from the War Office the Anglesey Barracks and the site of the Duke of York's Bastion of the Portsea defences which had been demolished in 1870–76. As this area was insufficient the former Garrison Hospital site within Townshend's Bastion on the south side of the then Queen's Road was also acquired for the Wardroom.

The new buildings of the barracks were built from 1899–1903 to the design of the Naval Works Loan Department headed by Colonel Sir Henry Pilkington RE. They were modelled on the stone RN Barracks at Devonport begun in 1879 and are virtually indistinguishable from those at Chatham except for the use of Doulting rather than Portland stone for the dressings to the brickwork.

The barracks has been extensively rebuilt in the 1960s and 70s but the most important older buildings survive. The barracks was originally styled HMS Victory but this was changed because of confusion with the ship. *H E Danreuther: 'The Royal Naval Barracks Portsmouth'. UCHB.*

Rodney Block, Royal Naval Barracks

Rodney Block, Grade II

1849–9, the retained soldiers' quarters of Anglesey Barracks. Originally a plain symmetrical classical 35 bay composition, the end three and central seven bays broken forward and the three bay centrepiece forward again. The sixteen left hand bays were bombed out in World War II and have been demolished. Three storeys, red brick with Portland stone plinth, first floor level band course, eaves cornice and coping to the now rendered parapet. The centrepiece is pedimented, with an oculus now open to the sky but formerly containing a relief. The parapet steps up above the pediment with a straight coping in the centre flanked by scrolls; this formerly supported a splendid stone lion which has been removed as it became insecure. Sash windows, triple on the first floor over the doorways, with gauged brick flat arches. Plain stone pilaster and entablature doorcases in the centre and every seventh bay to the sides.

Gymnasium

Late 19th C. Built as the Drill Hall of the Third Volunteer Battalion of the Hampshire Regiment, the Duke of Connaught's Own, but taken over for the RN Barracks. The large square hall has a double span iron truss roof and is enclosed within a two storey one room deep ring of ancillary spaces. Brick exterior with Doulting stone dressings, slate roofs. The Alfred Road frontage, threatened by Corporation road widening proposals, is an ambitious composition with pyramidal roofed central and flanking pavilions with attractive terracotta reliefs in the window tympana on both storeys. On the western angle is the clock tower, an imposing campanile with clasping angle pilasters, an arcaded 'belfry' stage above a strongly projecting cornice and a steep pyramidal copper roof which is a landmark to a formless part of the city.

Gymnasium, Royal Naval Barracks

PORTSMOUTH

ROYAL NAVAL BARRACKS

Main Gate

1899–1903. Rusticated Doulting stone vehicular archway flanked by smaller pedestrian arches. The four piers have alternate bands of stone and red brickwork. The central archway is enclosed by attached Ionic columns carrying an open segmental pediment. The tympanum has the Royal Arms and the keystone a naval crown and fouled anchor carved and painted in the vigorous style of ships' figureheads. The side arches are spanned by curious lintels at springing level and the outer piers carry steep pyramids on stone spheres.

Main Gate, Royal Naval Barracks

The gateway now sits isolated on a traffic island with its gates closed. The painted lion mounted incongruously on the modern guardhouse nearby is a survival of its predecessor.

Barham Block

1899-1903, the original Depot offices. A pleasant two storey slate roofed brick block with stone dressings which groups well with the adjacent Gymnasium and the Wardroom and the Roman Catholic Cathedral across the street.

Wardroom, Grade II

1899–1903. Across Queen Street from the main part of the barracks, a lively symmetrical composition of three storey centre and flank blocks with single storey links. Red brick with lavish Doulting stone dressings in Flemish classical style. The wardroom proper at the rear of the main block is a tremendous hammer beamed hall. Above the wainscotting is a series of paintings by H Wyhe of great naval victories including 'The Glorious First of June' and 'Copenhagen'. The relocated gateways have piers similar to the outer ones of the main gate.

Wardroom, Royal Naval Barracks

PORTSMOUTH

Landport Gate, St George's Road
MOD (Navy), Freehold
Ancient Monument

1760, the only one of the town gates of Portsmouth
and Portsea to remain in situ, though shorn of its
context of ramparts and ditches. The design is very
old-fashioned for its date, a square masonry block
with a rusticated segmental archway on each face.
The main elevation to the outside of the line of the
ramparts is crowned by a low square turret with an
octagonal stone cupola with a concave roof and ball
finial. The flank walls were originally largely
masked by the ramparts. In DOE Guardianship.

Landport Gate, Portsmouth

HMS VERNON, St George's Road
MOD (Navy), Freehold

A separate government department, the Board of
Ordnance, was responsible for all guns and
ammunition used by the Navy and Army until it
was abolished for inefficiency in 1855. Each major
Dockyard had its associated Gun Wharf and that at
Portsmouth is now the site of HMS Vernon. The
original wharf lay between the town and dockyard
on the north side of the Mill Road channel. The
Board purchased additional land on the south side
of the channel towards the end of the 18th C to
meet increasing demand for facilities. The present
camber perpetuates the line of the old channel.
Much rebuilding took place in the early 19th C
from which period the earliest surviving buildings
date. Certain of the architectural motifs used echo
Vanbrugh style Ordnance buildings elsewhere of a
century earlier. *UCHB, Coad.*

Former Gateway, New Ordnance Wharf

C1810. Red brick piers with round-headed recesses
and roundels on the faces. Elaborately moulded
stone caps surmounted by stone mortars. Now
bricked up; sections of original boundary wall with
blind arches remain on either side.

Grand Storehouse, HMS Vernon

PORTSMOUTH

HMS VERNON

Grand Storehouse or Vulcan Building, New Ordnance Wharf
Ancient Monument, Grade II

Begun in 1811 as a showpiece building far more monumental than the usual run of Ordnance buildings. Originally a great 'U' shaped pile on the axis of the gateway opening towards the wharfside, the guns being laid out in the open within the court. The north wing was destroyed by bombing and not rebuilt, the centre has suffered considerably from settlement.

The main east elevation was originally of fifteen bays, the three at each end broken forward twice and pedimented, the central five broken forward and the centre three again. Gauged brick flat arches to sash windows, lunette in the surviving pediment. Large entrance doors within two order gauged brick arch in central of end bays. The axial entrance passage has a rusticated stone archway within baseless Tuscan pillars and entablature. The plaque over is inscribed 'Major General Fisher, Commanding Royal Engineers, 1814'. The courtyard side of the central block has a matching archway. The three centre bays have a low false attic with stone panels surmounted by a pediment with a central oculus. The free end of the south wing is identical to its attached end.

The south elevation of this wing is a satisfying symmetrical composition in its own right. The three centre bays of the nine are treated in the same fashion as the end returns. At each end is a broken forward half bay with a blind arch on each storey. The roof was originally slated with plain lead covered dormers. The interior is divided by a brick spine wall and supported by cast iron columns. The very tall lower storey has a mezzanine between the spine wall and columns, presumably for storing gun carriages. Some of the original brick ground floor remains. The attic is carried on massive timber trusses. There was formerly a splendid cupola over the centres.

Building No 47, New Ordnance Wharf

C1810, a small rectangular two storey store house much more typical of Ordnance buildings than the Grand Store. Red brick with burnt headers. Bembridge stone plinth, projecting first floor level brick band course. Segmental headed sash windows, two large segmental archways in the north west end. Hipped slate roof. Much rebuilt, especially the parapet.

Grand Storehouse, HMS Vernon

Vernon Offices, HMS Vernon

Vernon Offices, Old Ordnance Wharf
Ancient Monument, Grade II

C1810, a well proportioned long rectangular two storey block. Red brick with burnt headers, Bembridge stone plinth, first floor level band course and cornice with brick dentilation. Fifteen bay front, the centre three broken forward and pedimented. Camber arches to sash windows, some windows in the end walls are oculi. Hipped slate roof behind parapet.

Sailing Centre, New Ordnance Wharf

C1810, built as a guard house beside the now vanished bridge between the New and Old Gunwharfs. A small single storey block, originally one square room in red brick with burnt headers; extended to the east in plain red brick. Brick dentil eaves to hipped tiled roof.

Walls and Gates, Grade II

1870s, to enclose the additional ground to the east taken in when the Portsmouth land defences were demolished and the Mill Pond filled in. The wall is red brick with stone plinth and coping and yellow brick panels with red brick diamond decoration. The now blocked gate in Gunwharf Road has massive stone piers and is overlooked by a corbelled out stone 'pulpit' with musketry loops. There is a simi-

Main Gate, HMS Vernon

lar pulpit on the angle of the wall at the junction of Gunwharf and St George's Roads.

The main gate is a weird mixture of classical symmetry and detail and mock medieval motifs and irregularity. Red brick with Portland stone dressings. Moulded three-centred roadway arch flanked by massive piers with pedestrian doorways with keystones and architrave surrounds. The right hand pier is larger and developed into a turret with mock machicolation and a crenellated parapet, with an elaborate weathervane. The archway and left hand pier are crowned with classical cornices. The upper portion of the gateway is liberally provided with rifle loops. The gates themselves are a fine piece of iron work.

PORTSMOUTH

**SPITHEAD FORTS, Horse Sand Fort,
No Man's Land Fort, St Helen's Fort
MOD (Navy)
Ancient Monuments**

The last two are strictly in the Isle of Wight but are described here for convenience.

1862–71, with Spitbank Fort, now in private hands; constructed by (later Sir) John Hawkshaw. Building of artillery towers on No Man's Land and Horse Sands Shoals either side of the deep water channel had been sanctioned prior to the 1859 Royal Commission. They recommended three additional towers, on Spitbank, between Horse Sands and Portsea Island and on Sturbridge Shoal. The first two were deleted for economy but when Sturbridge Shoal proved an inadequate foundation Spitbank was reinstated together with another fort on Ryde Sand, which also proving inadequate it was relocated off St Helen's Point.

While the foundations were being laid tests showed that masonry was unable to withstand the close range fire to which forts in the sea-way could be subjected and the designs were altered to provide armoured iron casemates where they were exposed to hostile naval guns. Like all fortifications of the period, their armament was obsolete almost as soon as it was installed; Horse Sand Fort was rearmed twice within a decade of first being armed in 1874. St Helen's was made obsolete by the construction of Nodes Point Battery on the shore behind c 1900, the others were armed until after the last war.

St Helen's Fort, Spithead

The two main forts, Horse Sand and No Man's Land, are of the same pattern above their massive raft foundations with a 100′ dia granite base to the armoured iron superstructure. Each mounted 49 heavy guns in two tiers of casemates and the roofs were reinforced to take five more in turret mountings which never were installed.

Spitbank Fort is 150′ dia with a single tier of casemates and armoured only on the seaward side. Nine heavy guns commanded the sea and seven lighter ones the Southsea beaches. St Helen's Fort is founded on a ring of iron caissons. Only the seaward side is armoured. Six heavy guns commanded the sea, two being mounted on turn tables so that by using two ports in the shield 60° apart and with their usual 60° traverse each could cover an arc of 120°. The landward side seems never to have received its four lighter guns. *AMS, Balfour, Hogg.*

Horse Sand Fort, Spithead

SOUTHAMPTON

1a Bugle Street, Southampton

1a Bugle Street
MOD (RAF), Leased
Grade II, Conservation Area

Built as the Yacht Club in 1846 by T S Hack, now occupied by the University Air Squadron. A fine painted stucco three storey building five bays square, in Italianate classical style. Rusticated quoins and ground floor, with an entablature over. Plaster surrounds to first floor windows with shell ornamented tympana. Small second floor windows between the massive paired brackets to the heavily projecting cornice. The front overlooking the pier has a deep first floor balcony supported on a Tuscan colonnade. The Bugle Street front has a fine central doorway. Hipped slate roof with corner chimney stacks and, on the pier front, a two bay attic above the central three bays. *UCHB, Pevsner.*

6, 7, 8 Carlton Crescent
Government Offices, Freehold
Grade II, Conservation Area

Three early 19th C houses, part of the most spectacular Regency development in Southampton. Three storeys and basement with lower linking blocks behind screen walls. Painted stucco fronts with rusticated ground floors and a giant order of shallow Doric pilasters through the first and second floors. Nos 6 and 7 are three bays wide, No 8 has an additional bay with a full height segmental bow. Sash windows with glazing bars; recessed doorways, No 8 with a Doric porch. Continuous first floor balconies with cast iron railings to Nos 7 and 8. The entablature and blocking course parapets conceal slate roofs. Cast iron area railings. The rear elevations are much altered. *UCHB, Pevsner.*

167

SOUTHAMPTON

6, 7, 8 Carlton Crescent, Southampton

County Court, Southampton

SOUTHAMPTON

County Court, Castle Square
Lord Chancellor's Department, Freehold
Grade II, Conservation Area

Built in 1851–53, the architect is unrecorded but possibly was T S Hack. An elaborate Italianate design with a large central feature and single storey wings. Yellow brickwork swamped by painted stucco cornices and window surrounds and heavily rusticated quoins. Royal Arms in the tympanum of the centrepiece.

FORMER ORDNANCE SURVEY HEADQUARTERS
London Road
Government Offices, Freehold
Grade II, Group Value, Conservation Area

The Ordnance Survey was established in 1791 in offices in the Tower of London which were destroyed by the fire there in 1841. There was fortuitously an empty cavalry barracks at Southampton, lately used as an asylum for soldiers' orphans, which became the new accommodation. The site was severely bombed in World War II and eventually completely evacuated in favour of Crabwood. The unlisted buildings on the site were demolished and redevelopment proposals are in hand. The northern part of the site, including the former Director General's House, has been disposed of.

The surviving group of mid 19th C buildings are generally similar in character, yellow brick with slate roofs, and mainly of two storeys. They have sash windows with glazing bars, some being triple lights and some with semi-circular heads with recessed stucco fan tympana. *UCHB.*

Entrance Block

At the south end of the site, an arched carriageway flanked by single storey wings. Stuccoed pilasters framing the archway and parapet band course. The parapet conceals the roof and has the Royal Arms set against the raised centre.

West Range

A two storey block with the ends and centre broken forward. Stuccoed first floor band course, dentil cornice and blocking course and surround to the central first floor window.

North Block

A free standing two storey pavilion, three bays square, with semi-circular headed ground floor windows. Pyramidal slate roof with dormers on some faces.

Crabwood House, Romsey Road
Ordnance Survey, Freehold
Grade III

An early 19th C two storey painted stucco house. Three by two bay main block with lower service wing to the north. Sash windows with glazing bars, canted ground floor bays on the south side. Doric porch in the centre of the east side, conservatory attached to the west side. Hipped slate roof with overhanging eaves. Used for social facilities for the new Ordnance Survey Headquarters building. *UCHB.*

Crabwood House, Southampton

SOUTHWICK

Southwick House, HMS Dryad

SOUTHWICK HOUSE, HMS Dryad
MOD (Navy), Freehold
Grade II

Rebuilt by 1841 after a fire in 1838 by Sidney Howell. The shell of the earlier house was apparently retained and given an additional storey. An imposing Italian renaissance style three storey painted stucco mansion. Quoined angles, rusticated ground floor, first and second floor sill level band courses, bracketed eaves cornice with blocking course. The main south garden front has a full height central three window bow with three windows on either side, the outer pairs broken forward slightly. The ground floor is fronted with an Ionic colonnade curving round the bow, with coupled columns to the straight runs except at the ends. The upper floor windows have architrave surrounds, with bracketed pediments, some segmental, on the first floor.

Five window east entrance front, the centre three closely spaced and broken forward, with a balustraded four column porte cochère matching the colonnade on the south front, both of which features were found on the earlier house. The north front has a central two storey three sided bay flanked by three storey sides. On the west side of the house is a large two storey service wing in similar but plainer style, with canted bays on the south side now largely

obscured by the modern dining room extension. The slate roofs are mainly concealed by the parapets.

The interior has a colonnaded passage from the entrance hall to the central stair hall which houses a cantilevered staircase under a lantern light. The house was General Eisenhower's HQ for the Normandy landings and the D-Day Map is preserved in the operations room.

Former Stable Block, Grade II

Early 19th C contemporary with the earlier house. Painted stucco 'L' shaped one and two storey block, much altered. Some arcading of elevations, slate roofs.

'Campanile'

Mid 19th C, slender square Italianate painted stucco tower with stages articulated by band courses. Battered rusticated ground stage with archway in each face. Shaft with two tall shallow arched panels and clock face rounded on each side. Two round headed windows on each face of upper stage. Elaborate corbel table cornice and shallow pyramidal lead roof.

TIDWORTH

MOD (Army), Freehold

The garrison straddles the county border, lying partly within North Tidworth (Wiltshire) but mainly within South Tidworth (Hampshire) and so is described under the latter county.

Tidworth Garrison was established in 1903 with barracks for eight battalions. The original buildings are mainly two storeyed, substantially built in hard red brick with sash windows and hipped slate roofs. The elaboration of the porches and eaves is proportional to their status. Unfortunately some have been re-roofed with concrete tiles.

The layout of the original barracks in a quadrant following the contours is well suited to the configuration of the ground and gives regularity without monotony. The standardisation of buildings and layout within each barracks provides unity while the changes in level and orientation give variety. The character of the garrison is formed as much by the generous grassed areas and extensive mature tree planting as by the buildings.

Tidworth Stable Block

A large slate roofed two storey brick block around a square courtyard, which has been butchered over the years by thoughtless alterations. The vertical hardwood cladding to the dumpy clock turret is particularly unfortumate.

Tidworth Lodge

Tidworth Lodge

A delightful single storey white painted brick cottage with a large oversailing hipped slate roof on rustic columns. Central doorway and multi-light casements. Tall brick central chimney stack.

St George and St Patrick (RC)

1912 by GLW Blount, a modest long low aisled rectangle of flint with limestone dressings, with a squat corner tower. Slate roofed.

Garrison Church of St Michael (C of E)

1912 by Douglas Hoyland, completely of terracotta. Basilican in section on a cruciform plan, including transept aisles. Lancet windows with foliated heads in square frames, mainly in triplets. Tiled roofs with a flèche over the crossing.

St Michael, Tidworth

WINCHESTER

4 The Close
Lord Chancellor's Department, Leased
Grade I, Group Value, Conservation Area

An L-shaped house. The main wing is late 17th-early 18th C, much altered, of two storeys. The seven bay brick front has a projecting three bay centre piece of red brick with stone quoins. The central bay is quoined with a pediment against the parapet and a modern porch. Sash windows except those to the left of the centrepiece which are cross-mullioned. Tiled roof.

The east wing is of two periods. The section forming the junction with the main block is rendered with an attic in the tiled roof. A late 18th C section with a slate roof projects into the Close.

The 18th C or earlier garden wall of tile coped flint, stone and brick is listed Grade II in its own right.

4 The Close, Winchester

PENINSULAR BARRACKS, Romsey Road
MOD (Army), Freehold
Ancient Monument (part), Conservation Area

The Barracks occupies what is after the Cathedral the most historic site in the city. The Knoll which forms the Upper Barracks was enclosed by a salient of the Roman wall before becoming the site of the medieval royal castle, the Great Hall of which survives in the adjacent County Court area, and is an Ancient Monument.

In 1683 construction began to the design of Sir Christopher Wren of a great palace intended to be the principal residence of Charles II outside London, but is was left a carcass on the King's death two years later. After various vicissitudes the 'King's House' was converted to Barracks in 1810 and in 1894 it was destroyed by fire. Most of the present barracks date from the subsequent rebuilding of 1899–1902 which incorporated some salvaged fragments of the palace. Between 1961–64 a major rebuilding took place in which the Officers' Mess and Married Quarters of 1810 were demolished and new buildings put in their place while the remaining buildings were remodelled internally. *UCHB, Pevsner, King's Works.*

Old Hospital Block

C1850, the only pre-fire building left in the Upper Barracks. A plain but effective three storey slate roofed brick block facing Romsey Road.

Garrison Church and School, Grade II

A strange mid 19th C building beside Southgate Street. Eleven bays long, wide and low with flint and brick walls with segmental arcading on pilasters. Pedimented gables to the slate roof which is carried on massive timber and iron queen-post trusses. A vestry with a plate traceried window was added on the north side and, c 1891, the brick apse and north porch. The school occupied the west end.

Garrison Church and School, Winchester

Colonnade Block, Grade II

An imposing single storey red brick block with heavy Portland stone dressings. It has a seven bay Roman Doric colonnade on the front with the entablature carried around the block and pedimented gables to the slate roof.

Colonnade Block, Peninsular Barracks

North West Block

The least pretentious of the c 1900 buildings in the Upper Barracks. Two storeys, red brick with minimal stone dressings. Pedimented centrepiece and gables to the slate roof.

North West Block, Peninsular Barracks

Long Block, Peninsular Barracks, Winchester

WINCHESTER   PENINSULAR BARRACKS

Short Block, Peninsular Barracks, Wichester

Long Block, Grade II

A monumental four storey 35 bay red brick block with extensive stone dressings. The centrepiece is a three bay portico of giant Composite attached columns three storeys high, flanked by open bays with pilasters and free standing columns, with a continuous attic storey and pediment with the Royal Arms, reusing stonework from the Palace. The wings each have a pair of three bay projecting pedimented features.

Short Block, Grade II

Repeats the general design of Long Block within thirteen bays. Matching three bay central feature, also with the Royal Arms in the pediment, but with hipped roofs to the two bay projecting terminations to the wings.

East Block, Grade II

Similar to but less elaborate than Long and Short Blocks. Two storeys only, fifteen bays with projecting centre and ends. Red brick with stone dressings, central pediment with a clock face in the tympanum; slate roof with a cupola.

Instruction (formerly Drill) Shed

The southern one of a pair flanking East Block. Red brick with stone dressings, colonnaded on the Parade Ground side; slate roofed. Its pair on the north side has been rebuilt with a raised roof for use as a gymnasium.

East Block, Peninsular Barracks, Winchester

WINCHESTER

Serle's House, Winchester

Serle's House, Southgate Street
MOD (Army), Freehold
Grade II*, Conservation Area

Functionally a part of the Peninsular Barracks but visually part of Southgate Street. A fine baroque mansion of c 1730, convincingly attributed to Thomas Archer. Three storeys, seven bay front, in high quality red brickwork. Giant Doric pilasters on pedestals the height of the ground floor are set in from the angles with an eaves entablature running all round. The centre bay of the garden front breaks forward with curved windowed return bays and pilasters with a segmental pediment set incongruously against an upswept brick parapet. The sash windows have keystoned segmental heads. The stone porch and doorcase were added in 1952.

The original street front at the rear is much plainer with an added porch with an almost neo-classical tetrastyle Tuscan portico. The rainwater heads are dated 1780 with the cypher of George III. The fine oval entrance hall contains an 'imperial' staircase leading to the principal first floor.

Serle's House, Winchester

The ground floor is the museum of the Royal Hampshire Regiment and the garden, including the modern walls, piers and gates to Southgate Street in matching style and listed Grade II, is their war memorial for which they are responsible. *UCHB, Pesvner, Country Life*.

COWES

Foresters Hall, 32 Sun Hill
MOD (Navy), DEP, Freehold
Grade II, Conservation Area

Mid 19th Century, free classical style painted stucco three bay facade, two storeys with superimposed orders of pilasters. Rusticated ground floor with deep central archway surmounted by a segmental pediment. Balustraded parapet with pedimented sculptured panel in the centre. *UCHB.*

EAST COWES

OSBORNE HOUSE, Whippingham Road
Department of the Environment, Freehold
Grade I, Group Value, Area of Outstanding Natural Beauty

When Queen Victoria and Prince Albert were married in 1840 there was no royal residence in which they could enjoy family life free from state ceremonial and away from the public eye. The Osborne estate was at first leased and eventually purchased as the Queen's private property from Lady Isabella Blackford in 1845. The existing 18th C house was too small and construction of the present Osborne House began immediately.

Osborne House

EAST COWES　　　　　　　　　　　　　　　　　　　　　　OSBORNE HOUSE

No architect was employed, the design being worked out between Prince Albert and the London builder Thomas Cubitt, best known as the developer of Belgravia and Pimlico. The result has to be judged a success both in terms of planning and appearance, enjoying as it does a superb site overlooking the Solent. The house is in the Italianate classical style to which Cubbitt's name is inseperably attached. It is of rendered brickwork, incorporating the most modern methods of construction including cast iron beams, and intended to be fire proof.

The central Pavilion was the first part to be built, being occupied in 1846. It is a basically square three storey block with the rooms planned around a central stairhall rising the full height and decorated with Dyce's mural painting of Neptune entrusting the Command of the Sea to Britannia. The state rooms on the ground floor form a sequence of linked spaces; the private apartments are on the first floor. Beside the entrance porch is the 107 foot high Flag Tower.

In 1848 work began on the U-shaped Main Wing and Household Wing on the right side of the entr-ance court, completed in 1851. Also mainly three storeys, linked to the Pavilion by a two storey arcaded loggia, enclosed on the ground floor. At the eastern end of the north front is the 90 foot tall Clock Tower balancing the Flag Tower.

The Durbar Wing was added on the left of the entrance court in 1890 to provide a large hall for receptions. The Indian style was chosen and its execution entrusted to Bhai Ram Singh and John Lockwood Kipling, father of Rudyard Kipling. The exterior however perpetuates Cubitt's style.

Queen Victoria died at Osborne in 1901 and Edward VII presented most of the estate to the nation. The Main and Household Wings became a convalescent home and in 1904 the state apartments and part of the grounds were opened to the public. In 1954 the private apartments, virtually unchanged since the death of Prince Albert at Windsor in 1861, were opened to the public also. *UCHB, Pevsner, Colvin, J Charlton 'Osborne House', H Hobhouse: 'Thomas Cubitt, Master Builder', T Whittle: 'Victoria and Albert at Home'.*

Durbar Room, Osborne House

EAST COWES   OSBORNE HOUSE

Central Hall, Osborne House

Andromeda, Osborne House

Terraces, Alcoves, Statues and Fountains
Grade II, Group Value

Forming an integral part of the house and built concurrently in 1847-54. An elaborate series of balustraded terraces and staircases leading down to the way to the sea shore, with a shell-roofed alcove and a mass of statuary. The Venus and Andromeda fountains were designed by Ludwig Grüner. The statue of Andromeda is by John Bell and was bought from the Great Exhibition of 1851.

Porch from Old Osborne House, Grade II

The 18th C Osborne House was demolished at the end of 1847 to permit the construction of the Household Wing. The entrance porch was salvaged and reconstructed as the main entrance to the walled garden.

Fort Albert, Osborne House

Prince of Wales Gates and Lodge, Grade II, Group Value

After 1845, by Thomas Cubitt. Two storey T-shaped lodge in cement rendered Italianate style with rusticated quoins on ground floor and first floor band course. Shallow pitched slate roof with deep eaves and gable projections. Canted ground floor bay at west end and arcaded loggia in south west angle, both with bracketed cornice and blocking course. Ornate pyramidal cast iron gate piers and cast iron railings.

178

EAST COWES   OSBORNE HOUSE

Swiss Cottage, Osborne House

The Swiss Cottage, Grade II, Group Value

The focus of a group of buildings sited half a mile to the east of the house. A prefabricated timber chalet imported from Switzerland and put up in 1853–54. A two storey structure of interlocking horizontal squared baulks with a fretted balcony around the first floor and deep over-hanging eaves. It was intended for the practical education of the royal children, with a fully equipped kitchen on the ground floor below the living rooms.

Swiss Cottage Museum, Grade II, Group Value

Built nearby in 1862 to house the collections of curiosities made by the royal children. The interior has a triple aisled timber frame.

Toolshed, Grade II, Group Value

C1860. A simple thatch-roofed weather boarded open sided shed built to house the individual gardening tools and wheel barrows of the royal children.

Quite as substantial as the toolshed though not a building is Queen Victoria's bathing machine which is preserved nearby.

Fort Albert, Grade II, Group Value

A miniature earth fort with a bastioned trace and brick guard room. Built in 1860 for Prince Arthur, later Field Marshal the Duke of Connaught.

Swiss Cottage Museum, Osborne House

179

NEWPORT

36 Carisbrooke Road
DHSS, Hired
Grade II

With Nos 26–80 (even), part of a mid 19th C Italianate style terrace.

Three storey stuccoed fronts with channelled ground floor, first floor level band course, moulded second floor sill level band and bracketed cornice to shallow pitched slate roof. Architrave surrounds to ground and second floor windows. First floors have alternating fenestration of three-sided bays or two pedimented windows, one segmental, the other straight, linked by bracketed cast iron balconies. Paired semi-circular headed doorways.

20 Holyrood Street
Customs and Excise, Leased
Grade II, Group Value, Conservation Area

A tall early 19th C house. Three storey three window front of grey brick headers with red brick dressings. Sash windows, with glazing bard intact and blind boxes on upper storeys. Semi-circular headed doorway with fan-light. *UCHB*.

Broadlands, 3 Staplers Road
Government Offices, Freehold

The earliest part is an early 19th C three storey block, three bays by four, yellow stock brick with a thin Portland stone plinth and first and second floor level band courses. Gauged brick flat arches to sash windows. The side bay of the entrance, south elevation have blind windows below the (curtailed) chimney stacks. In the centre is a plain stone porch with coupled pilasters. Hipped slate roof with deep eaves. The ground floor of the east elevation has been rendered and is chewed up by inserted windows. This original part is almost overwhelmed by subsequent extensions.

Broadlands, Newport

BOUGHTON MONCHELSEA

Wierton Grange
Lord Chancellor's Department, Freehold

A comfortable late Victorian house in a rural setting, dated 1896 on a rainwater head. Two storeys
and attic, red brick with occasional stone dressings,
tile hanging on the upper storeys, timber mullion
and transom windows with leaded lights. Massive
steeply-pitched tiled roofs, the central one surmounted by a cupolaed look out, and tall chimney
stacks. The entrance front is an unresolved jumble
but the garden front is a basically symmetrical composition with canted two storey bays and
pedimented dormers. The interiors are spacious
and well lit, with a galleried two storey hall and
much fine joinery.

Wierton Grange, Boughton Monchelsea

CANTERBURY

Sessions House, Langport Street
Lord Chancellor's Department, Freehold
Grade II, Group Value, Conservation Area

1808–10 by George Byfield, immediately after the
adjacent prison. An austere cubical neo-classical
block with a very fine Portland stone ashlar front of
two storeys, five windows, the central bay with giant
attached Doric columns in antis. Cornice and blocking course, the central entablature with high relief
symbols of justice and authority. Six-panelled double doors and rectangular fanlight within plain
doorcase with bracketed cornice. The proportions of
the front have been spoiled by two small extensions
on the end and the much larger addition at the rear
relates uneasily.

The contemporary walls and railings are listed in

Sessions House, Canterbury

their own right. The red brick dwarf wall with a
stone coping is surmounted by wrought iron spear
railings with main standards in the form of fasces.
Three pairs of wrought iron gates. *UCHB, Pevsner.*

CHATHAM

Former Guardroom, Kitchener Barracks,
Brompton Hill
MOD (Army), Freehold

Early 18th C. Two storeys, lower ground floor and
attic, four window front. Stock brick with plinth, first
floor and parapet level band courses, gauged brick
camber arches to sash windows with glazing bars.
Steeply pitched roof, now slated, with lead flat on top.

Former Guardroom, Kitchener Barracks

CHATHAM

Brompton Lines
MOD (Army), Freehold
Ancient Monument, Conservation Area

Built in 1756 by Hugh Debbieg on the high ground overlooking the dockyard to protect it from land attack. A regular bastioned trace with a brick revetted scarp and counterscarp. Sections of the rampart have been flattened and parts of the ditch filled in.

The lines were reconstructed in 1778. At the southern end the provision of the 'Couvre Port', Spur Battery and Prince William's Bastion and retrenchments to form Amhurst Redoubt and Belvedere Battery created an immensely strong position, which was sold to the Fort Amhurst Trust in 1982 for restoration and opening to the public. Townshend's Redoubt, a similar construction at the northern end of the lines has largely disappeared.

Lord Kitchener, Chatham

Statue of Lord Kitchener, Dock Road
Grade II

Bronze equestrian statue in military dress on a pitched faced Portland stone ashlar plinth. A replica of the statue at the Maidan, Calcutta, it was erected in front of the Sudan Defence Forces HQ, Khartoum, in 1921 and moved to Chatham in 1960.

Garrison Church, Maxwell Road, Brompton
MOD (Army), Freehold
Conservation Area

1857, Kentish ragstone rubble with Bath stone dressings, slate roofs. Seven bay nave, without clerestory, and aisles with flying buttresses on spur walls, set diagonally at the corners. Aisleless chancel with organ chamber and vestry on north side and porch in angle with south aisle. Small western porch and bellcote on west gable. Mainly plate traceried windows. Spacious interior with open timber arch braced truss roof on cast iron arcade columns.

Garrison Church, Brompton

CHATHAM

BROMPTON BARRACKS, Wood Street
MOD (Army), Freehold
Conservation Area

The barracks were begun in 1804 for the Royal Artillery garrisoning Chatham Lines. In 1856 they were made over to the Royal Engineers. The original buildings of 1804–06 designed by Lieut Col R D'Arcy surround the tree lined parade ground on three sides. *AMS, Pevsner.*

Main Block, Ancient Monument

1804–06, closing the west side of the parade ground. Two storeys, stock brick with Portland stone cornices and blocking course. Thirty one bay front articulated 7:6:5:6:7 with centre and ends broken forward and attic storeys forming turrets of their outer bays. Two giant Tuscan columns in antis with balustraded entablature front a rusticated ashlar faced recessed portico.

Generally gauged brick camber arches to sash windows with glazing bars. Triple windows with brick spandrels to segmental heads on ground floor of turrets. Semi-circular heads to central doorway and flanking windows. Rusticated stone surrounds to semi-circular headed doorways in penultimate bays of end and link sections. Slate roof, hipped on turrets.

North and South Blocks, Ancient Monuments

1804–06, facing each other across the parade ground. Very similar to the Main Block. Thirty five bay front with matching five bay centre piece and three storey end bays.

In the centre of North Block is the former chapel, now the museum of the Royal Engineers. Seven aisled bays with a segmental plaster barrel vault, semi-domed over the first two bays of the west end (liturgically, actually south). Bays 4, 5 and 6 arcaded with cross-vaults intersecting the main one. Very low semi-circular headed windows. The galleries have been curtailed over the aisles, opened up into the back corners and a re-entrant formed in the centre.

Study Centre and North East Block, Ancient Monuments

1861, framing the open east side of the parade ground. Two storeys, stock brick, five bay centres with three bay wings, sash windows, hipped slate roofs. The Study Centre to the south has an arcaded centre and has been extended on its east side.

Main Block, Brompton Barracks, Chatham

CHATHAM

BROMPTON BARRACKS

Institute Building, Brompton Barracks, Chatham

Institute Building, Ancient Monument

1872–74 by Lieut F Ommaney, closing the axis to the east of the parade ground. Two storeys, grey brick with extensive pale terracotta ornament. Twenty five closely spaced window bays on front with paired bays broken forward at the ends and either side of the three bay centre, which has a recessed portico at first floor level with coupled Corinthian columns. The ground floor and quoins on the first floor are rusticated with dog-toothed bands. Semi-circular heads to ground floor windows, segmental to first floor. Richly ornamented entablature with modillion cornice and balustraded parapet over centre and ends. Hipped slate roof.

(Royal Engineer Memorials, Ancient Monuments)

No account of the Brompton Barracks can be complete without mention of the file of monuments which links the Institute Building to the Parade Ground, although they are the responsibility of the Institution of Royal Engineers and not of the Government. They are the triple arched Crimean War memorial, by Matthew Digby Wyatt, the Boer War memorial arch and the Great War memorial obelisk, together with the statue of General Gordon.

Ravelin Building

1904–07 by Major E C S Moore, built as the Electrical School. A large two storey block around an inner quadrangle, in unhistoric Edwardian style. Red brick with Portland stone dressings, with a curious grid of major and minor pilasters, string courses and cornices. The angles break forward to form towers and the main entrance is flanked by projecting three storey towers, all with domed cupolas.

Gymnasium

1860's, a T-shaped grey brick block with a porch in the centre of the head. Rundbogenstil arcaded elevations, circular windows in gables, corbel table eaves. Tiled roofs with a large timber lantern with pyramidal roof over the junction. Across Wood Street from the main part of the barracks.

Gymnasium, Brompton Barracks

Ravelin Building, Brompton Barracks

CRANBROOK

Clermont, High Street
Department of Employment, Freehold
Grade II, Conservation Area

A late 19th C three storey three window wide painted brick front. Sash windows with glazing bars, two angled bays on the ground floor. Central porch with fluted capitals to columns and pilasters, open pediment, semi-circular fanlight and six-panel door. Half hipped tiled roof above timber modillion cornice. Tile-hung gable walls. An important building in a fine street. *UCHB.*

Clermont, Cranbrook

DARTFORD

County Court, Spital Street
Lord Chancellor's Department, Freehold
Grade II, Group Value

C1858, a modest two storey building with its principal, south, five bay white brick facade to Spital Street. Rusticated quoins and centre bay. Gauged brick arches with keystones and shaped surrounds, round-headed on the ground floor, segmental above. Central doorway with carved stone Royal Arms over. Stone modillion cornice and hipped slate roof. Irregularly windowed east return to Kent Road, yellow stock brick with white brick dressings. Some rear additions. The interior much altered but with the original plain stairway on the east side.

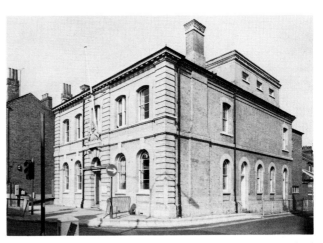

County Court, Dartford

DEAL

The Limes, 6 Broad Street
Department of Employment, Leased
Grade II, Group Value, Conservation Area

Early 19th C. Plain three storey red brick front, four windows in widely separated pairs with blank wall over central doorway. Flush sashes, glazing bars missing on the ground floor. Large doorcase with pilasters and entablature. Hipped tiled roof. *UCHB.*

The Limes, Deal

DEAL

ROYAL MARINE BARRACKS
MOD (Navy), Freehold

The barracks originated in the early 1790s with the building of North and South Barracks for Army use. East Barracks was begun in 1812 as a Naval Hospital on the site of an earlier hospital. The Marines did not arrive permanently until 1861. *UCHB.*

Administration Block, South Barracks

Administration Block, South Barracks

C1795, built as a stable/barracks block for a squadron of cavalry. Two storeys, stock brick, nine bays by three, the end pairs broken slightly forward. Gauged brick arches, mainly segmental, but semicircular at the ground floor ends, over mainly triple sash windows with glazing bars. Hipped slate roof with lead dressings. Like the similar building at Christchurch, Dorset, it has been much altered internally and externally.

Officers' Mess, South Barracks, Grade II

Early 19th C three storeys and attic, stock brick. Thirteen bay front with three bays added at each end in the mid 19th C. The central seven bays are broken forward and pedimented. Sash windows, glazing bars missing on ground floor, alternate windows on upper floors blind. Two projecting pedimented porches in outer bays of centre piece with round headed six-panel doors. Hipped slate roof with dormers. Square timber louvre over the pediment.

Garrison Church, South Barracks

St George's Garrison Church, South Barracks

Foundation stone laid 1905, dedicated 1907. The standard design also used at Eastney RM Barracks and the RN Barracks at Chatham and Devonport. It replaced the church of 1858 in North Barracks now used as a concert hall.

Officers' Mess, South Barracks, Deal

School of Music, East Barracks, Deal

1-4 Royal Buildings, East Barracks, Deal

School of Music (Former Infirmary), East Barracks
Grade II, Group Value

1812, yellow stock brick. Three storey, 27 bay front, the centre seven bays and end pairs broken forward. The central three bays project further and are pedimented with a broad segmental arch in the tympanum. Gauged brick flat arches to sash windows with glazing bars. Deeply projecting Tuscan porch with paired columns and pilasters. Moulded eaves cornice to hipped slate roof. Circular Tuscan cupola on square clock tower over pediment. At the rear is a tall narrow five bay building in similar style with a hipped slate roof.

1-4 Royal Buildings, East Barracks

Early 19th C. Two linked pairs of officers' houses. Three storeys and attic, four window front to each pair. Yellow stock brick, first floor sill level band course, modillion eaves cornice with blocking course. Semi-circular heads to ground floor windows. Sashes with reduced glazing bars. Slate mansard roofs with dormers. No 3 and 4 have been combined into one house and two three-sided bays formed on the first floor of No 4.

Walls and Gates at School of Music, East Barracks
Grade II, Group Value

Early 19th C stock brick forecourt wall about 10 foot high with piers at regular intervals, stone coping and capstones. The gates have cast iron spearhead railings and piers decorated with anchors and spy-glasses.

North Barracks

Largely rebuilt in the 1950s. The houses along North Barracks Road and the adjacent gate buildings are much altered survivors of an earlier period.

School of Music, East Barracks, Deal

187

DOVER

St Mary in Castro, Dover Castle, Castle Hill
MOD (Army), Freehold

The church of St Mary in Castro, dating from
c 1000, is the oldest occupied Government building.
Cruciform on plan, with a nave the same width as
the central tower and narrower chancel and 'trans-
epts' which originally only had much narrower
openings to the crossing. The church was considerably altered by Henry III. By the 18th C it was
derelict and roofless and used as a coal store. Restored sympathetically by Scott in 1862 and less sen-
sitively by Butterfield in 1888, who completed the
tower and added the vestry and the mosaic on the
lower part of the walls. *Guide, Pevsner, King's Works.*

Fort Burgoyne, Connaught Barracks
MOD (Army), Freehold
Ancient Monument

1861–68, built on the recommendation of the 1859
Royal Commission on the Defence of the United
Kingdom. Originally known as Castle Hill Fort.
Sited on Edinburgh Hill half a mile north of the
castle, it defends the eastern landward side of the
port and the only relatively level approach to the
castle. Two wing batteries at the rear cover the
south side, secured independently by ditches and
connected by lines to the main fort.

The fort itself forms a casemated barracks within
a polygonal trace. The ditches are flanked by one
double and three single caponiers, all of two tiers.
The gorge ditch forms a re-entrant angle with case-

St Mary in Castro, Dover

mated flanks for guns and musketry. Twenty nine
guns could be mounted on the ramparts, six in
paired Haxo casemates. There was a chemin des
rondes as well as a covered way. The conception of
the defences is such that if captured the fort would
be untenable against fire from the castle. *AMS.*

Fort Burgoyne, Dover

DOVER

Great Farthingloe Farmhouse, Dover

Great Farthingloe Farmhouse, Folkestone Road
MOD (Army), Freehold
Grade II, Area of Outstanding Natural Beauty

Three storey early 19th C house. Three window
pale yellow brick east front with flint plinth and
stone offset. Three sided bays on ground floor,
sashes above. Central door case with plain pilasters,
open pediment and semi-circular fanlight. Sides and
back flint and red brick. Hipped tiled roof. Large
rear extension.

The thatched barn to the west is of similar period
but incorporates reused timbers of an earlier date.
UCHB.

11 King Street
Manpower Services Commission, Freehold

Built as the Head Post Office, dated 1892 in the
gable. Three storeys, basement and attic, with a tall
ornamental terracotta main facade, now painted, of
four narrow bays in Jacobean style.

11 King Street, Dover

DOVER

Duke of York's Royal Military School, Guston
MOD (Army), DOE Freehold
Grade II, Group Value

1909 by Sir Henry Tanner, to house the school for sons of soldiers originally established in the Duke of York's Headquarters at Chelsea.

Sited on the high downland plateau north of the castle. Formal large scale layout; the road between the two pairs of entrance lodges forms the chord of a segment with the lesser buildings laid out along it and the corresponding arc, on either side of the main buildings which are on the central cross axis.

The buildings are in an informal arts and crafts style, mainly single storey, rough cast and red brick walls, much white painted joinery including sash windows and deep corniced eaves, with tiled roofs and numerous lead cupolas. The main buildings are the Chapel, with mixed brick and stone work, the former assembly hall, now the library, and the dining hall.

Some of the modern buildings on the site are of quite incredible insensitivity to their setting. *Pevsner*.

Duke of York's Royal Military School, Dover

GRAVESEND

Custom House, Gravesend

CUSTOM HOUSE, Commercial Place
Customs and Excise, Home Office, Freehold
Grade II

One of the oldest Customs establishments in the country, due to the town's position at the entrance to the Port of London. The first known appointment of a Gravesend man as 'Searcher' was made in 1356. The present Custom House, successor to several earlier ones, is a bold yellow brick three storey domestic-looking building of 1815–16. Main five bay south front to the Terrace, with a three bay return on the east, the latter with round-headed upper windows. Two set-back bays on the west side (probably of slightly different date), with blind openings and a Tuscan portico. Slightly projecting main entrance with renewed Royal Arms over (the original is in the garden); this leads to a tunnel-vaulted passage dividing the house. At the rear a two bay wing projects slightly each side of this passage; the west block (set back on the front) comes forward in a three bay curve. Most of the sash windows are original, without 'horns'. On top, concealed from the front bay by massive chimney stacks, is a bow-windowed look-out. Three cantilevered stone stairs, the principal one with restrained ornament in its iron balustrade. Extensive cellars. The doors and other internal joinery are largely original thoughout.

Long rear yard with substantial longitudinal dividing wall; harness room, boat-house and other utilitarian buildings, some two storeyed. George III cyphers on rainwater heads, etc. 'New' tile-hung boat-house 1875. *UCHB*.

Gazebo in the grounds, Grade II

Earlier than the house, probably c 1790; reputed to be a press-gang look-out. Octagonal, white weatherboarded, with simple pilasters at angles. Slate roof and octagonal brick chimney. Wooden internal stair to upper level. On the river wall and destined to be outside the flood wall now being built.

Gazebo, Custom House, Gravesend

191

HALSTEAD

**Fort Halstead, Royal Armaments Research and
Development Establishment**
MOD (Procurement Executive), Freehold
Ancient Monument

The London Defence Positions were established in
the 1890s to protect the capital from the most likely
directions of attack. To the south the line follows
the top of the South Downs escarpment from west
of Guildford to the west side of the Darent valley
where it turns north to meet the Thames at Dartford. Fort Halstead occupies the key position at the
south end of the Darent valley.

A chain of 'mobilisation centres', essentially store
houses protected against bombardment with a limited capability for self-defence, was established. In
the event of an invasion these would have been
linked by entrenchments and the line defended by
batteries of field artillery. Some of the positions
took on more of the nature of fully developed forts
capable of independent resistance. Fort Halstead is
of this type, costing indeed nearly twice as much as
the next most expensive and considerable larger.

It is an irregular eleven sided polygon about 200
yards across, with the original entrance in a re-
entrant on the north side. The earth rampart has a
parapet, banquette and terreplein, the ditch has a
concrete revetted scarp and sloping earth counterscarp. The rampart line is divided by four earth
traverses, three incorporating expense magazines. A
large central traverse running from the north side
divides the fort approximately into halves, having a
large magazine within it. A range of casemates is
built against the west rampart with a small arms
magazine in the bank. The structures are brick and
concrete.

The plans show gun emplacements but these do
not seem to have been provided and the fort would
have been defended by field pieces on the terreplein and riflemen on the banquette. The system of
defence positions was abandoned in 1906. Fort Halstead was a munitions depot in World War I, was
sold off in 1922 but was re-purchased in 1937.

The Fort is of great historical interest as a well
preserved example of the final phase in the development of permanent fortification, the last link
in a chain which begins with Iron Age hill forts,
which it more closely resembles in many respects
than any of the intervening phases. *Brigadier JRE
Hamilton-Bailie : 'Fort Halstead of the London Defence
Positions'; Fort 3.*

HYTHE

Martello Towers Nos 14 and 15
MOD (Army), Freehold
Ancient Monuments, Grade II

1806, part of the system of coastal defence against
invasion from Napoleonic France. Two storey circular brick towers. Parapeted gun platform carried on
a ring vault on the central pillar. Vaulted magazine
in the basement; the remainder of the flooring was
timber. Skin of Flemish bond facing brick set flush
with the masonry coping and door surrounds in
place of the usual rendered finish. The entrance
level windows have been widened and the splayed
embrasures cut back for Bren-gun positions in the last
war. The entrances are bricked up.

The line of Martello Towers was spaced and sited
to provide mutual support. No 13 survives in private hands just outside the range area. Nos 16 to 19
stood within the MOD area but except for No 19
had been destroyed by the sea by World War II. No
19 collapsed some years ago and lies strewn across
the beach giving an interesting insight into the details of its construction. Nos 14 and 15 were then
underpinned to prevent similar collapse but remain
dangerously close to the sea. *AMS, UCHB, Sutcliffe.*

Dymchurch Redoubt
MOD (Army), Freehold
Ancient Monument

1806, intended with its twin at Eastbourne as a
strong point in the line of Martello Towers constructed along the coast against the threat of invasion from Napoleonic France. Massive ringwork of
brick and stone sunk to parapet level in a deep and
wide brick revetted ditch. The central parade is surrounded by parabolic barrel vaulted casemates, surmounted by alternating embrasures for 24 pounders on traversing carriages and infantry banquettes.
Five caponiers traverse the ditch and the entrance
was via a draw-bridge. *Sutcliffe.*

MAIDSTONE

5 Clarendon Place, King Street
MOD (Army), Freehold
Grade II, Group Value, Conservation Area

With 1–7, a terrace of c 1830–40, three storeys and basement, brown brick. Nos 5 and 7 form a handed pair with two window bows flanking shared central windows. First floor sill level string course, cornice with blocking course. Sash windows, glazing bars missing on lower sashes of ground floor. Conjoined doorways with three Tuscan columns and entablature. *UCHB*.

5 Clarendon Place, Maidstone

MARGATE

Hawley Towers, 38 Hawley Square
MOD (Navy), Freehold
Grade II, Group Value, Conservation Area

On the south side of the fine Georgian square. Late 18th/early 19th C reconstruction of an earlier building. Somewhat irregularly fenestrated two storey centre with sash windows, flanked by three storey towers with two centre headed 'gothick' casements on the first and second floors, round headed doorway with cast fanlight and panelled door. Band courses and crenellated parapets, continued on the return end onto Churchfield Place. Painted brick, the west tower rendered, flint with brick dressings at the rear. *UCHB*.

Hawley Towers, Margate

RAMSGATE

Custom House, Harbour Parade
Customs & Excise, Freehold
Grade II, Conservation Area

1894, deep red brick with matching terracotta dressings in classical style. Two storeys, five bay facade, the centre three broken forward, with superimposed columns, Balustraded first floor level entablature and parapet. Surmounted by a copper dome and lantern. *UCHB*.

ROCHESTER

5 Castle Hill
Department of Health, Leased
Conservation Area

Late 19th C, one of the row of elaborate mansions which encloses the north side of the castle. Three storeys, basement and attic. Yellow stock brick almost submerged by lavish stone classical dressings. No two windows are alike.

SANDWICH

11 Market Street
Manpower Services Commission, Freehold
Conservation Area

Neo-Georgian but occupying an important position in the streetscape. A tall single storey and high attic. Red brick with Portland stone plinth, doorcase, ornamental band courses and cornice, balustraded centre section to the parapet and coping. Carved panels in the attic. Gauged brick arch to the large central doorway and flat arches to small flanking windows. Roof concealed by the parapet. Fine plaster dome to the former banking hall inside.

11 Market Street, Sandwich

SEVENOAKS

Boswell House, 41–44 London Road
Government Offices, Leased
Grade II, Conservation Area

Dated 1818, the first building designed by C R Cockerell, the great neo-classical architect. Built for Lady Boswell's Charity School on a budget of £500. The two storey, three bay pedimented centre is set forward slightly from the originally single storeyed end bays. Wealden sandstone, the ground floor ashlar with arched openings and rubble panels under windows. Ashlar band courses at first floor and first floor sill level; ashlar first floor quoins, windows and pediment, rubble walling and tympanum. Carved inscription and coat of arms in the pediment. The end bays have been raised in disparate fashion, one in rubble, the other is ashlar, both with rubble parapet walls with string course, coping and ball finials

Boswell House, Sevenoaks

on the corners. The flank walls are rubble with ashlar dressings with an arcaded ground floor. Windows and doors are modern. *UCHB.*

194

SHORNCLIFFE

Martello Towers Nos 6, 7, 9
MOD (Army) Freehold
Ancient Monuments, No 6 Conservation Area

1806, part of the system of coastal defence against invasion from Napoleonic France. Two storey circular brick towers, rendered. Parapeted gun platform carried on a ring vault on the central pillar. Vaulted magazine in the basement, the remainder of the floor was timber, some fragments survive. Stone coping and door surrounds. Set high on the cliffs, these towers all have deep dry moats, Nos 6 and 9 with brick counter scarp walls, No 7 with massive pitched face masonry. *AMS, Sutcliffe.*

TUNBRIDGE WELLS

63 Calverley Road, Tunbridge Wells

63 Calverley Road
MOD (Army), Freehold
Grade II, Group Value, Conservation Area

With No 61 one of several originally separate groups of neo-classical houses along the street, c 1835 by Decimus Burton, now linked by later in-filling. Nos 61 and 63 originally formed a four window front of three storeys and basement, the top storey a low attic above a plain band course, crowned with a moulded cornice and pedimented over the two central bays. Wealden sandstone ashlar facades, painted on No 63, which has a two-storey single bay extension linking it with No 65. Sash windows with glazing bars, the windows of No 63 have not been enlarged and in the attic are very small indeed. *UCHB.*

BANBURY

41 South Bar Street
Customs and Excise, Leased
Grade II, Conservation Area

Early 19th C. Three storey stuccoed front with quoins
and parapet, three windows wide, the centre ones
blind and flanked by pilasters. Bay windows on the
ground floor. Six panelled doorway with semi-circular
fanlight.

41 South Bar Street, Banbury

HENLEY

Dominion House, 5 Gravel Hill
Department of Transport, Part Hired
Grade II, Group Value

Early 19th C, three storey red brick building, the front
elevation painted. Semi-circular headed central doorway with canted bay shop window to the right. Some
late timber framing is visible in the partition wall of the
vehicular passage to the left. Two wide sash windows
on each upper storey. Deep eaves with paired brackets
to hipped slate roof.

OXFORD

Former Cowley Barracks Officers' Mess
Home Office, Freehold

Mid 19th C block, two storeys and attic, coursed
limestone rubble with ashlar banding and dressings to
mullioned and transomed sash windows. Hipped and
coped gabled single-lap tiled roofs, recently recovered.
Refurbished as offices with a sympathetic extension.

Former Cowley Barracks Officers' Mess, Oxford

OXFORD

Probate Registry, Oxford

Probate Registry, 10a New Road
Lord Chancellor's Department, Freehold
Grade II, Conservation Area

1864 by C Buckeridge in plate traceried ecclestiastical gothic style but with transomed windows. Compact two storey block with two pairs of gabled roofs set at right angles. Coursed rubble walling with ashlar dressings, red tiled roofs, masonry chimney stacks. Dwarf boundary wall and gate piers to match. *UCHB.*

35 St Giles
Tri-Service Careers Office, Leased
Grade II, Group Value, Conservation Area

The centre of a short early 19th C three house terrace each three windows wide. Three storeys, basement and attic. Fine ashlar front, rusticated ground floor with arched sash windows and doorway. Moulded surrounds to tall first floor windows with continuous iron balcony. Plain second floor windows with sill band. Moulded cornice and parapet with balustraded panels. Semi-circular headed dormers in slate mansard roof. The interior is reasonably intact. *UCHB, Pevsner.*

35 St Giles, Oxford

SHRIVENHAM

Becket Hall, Shrivenham

BECKETT HALL, Royal Military College of Science
MOD (Army), Freehold
Grade II

Beckett Lodge, Shrivenham

1831–34 by W D Atkinson for the sixth Viscount
Barrington, with a considerable amateur contribution
from his brother-in-law The Hon Thomas Liddell.
Two storeys and attic in a substantial and scholarly
Tudor style. Coursed rubble with ashlar dressings,
mullioned and transomed windows with a variety of
oriels and bays, crenellated parapets and stone roof.
An attractive skyline of pinnacled gables, rows of tall
chimney stacks, dormers and turrets.

    The main feature of the interior is the galleried
central hall rising through the full height of the house
and top lit. When the College moved from Woolwich
in 1947 the Hall became the Officers' Mess; it is now
used as the library. *UCHB, Pevsner, Colvin.*

Beckett Lodge

Single storey stone lodge with stone roof, contemporary with Beckett Hall. Adjacent to fine iron gates.

WALLINGFORD

22 St Mary's Street
Department of Employment, Hired
Grade II, Group Value, Conservation Area

Late 18th C house, two storeys and attic, grey brick with red dressings. Shop front with central late 18th C pedimented doorcase. Sash windows with near flush frames on the first floor, retaining their glazing bars. Timber modillion eaves cornice, tiled roof with small gabled dormers. *UCHB*.

WITNEY

28 Bridge Street
Government Offices, Freehold
Grade II, Conservation Area

Mid 19th C, originally a court house. A single storey five bay classical style front of considerable elaboration, arcaded with the doorway in the rusticated centre bay, heavy modillion cornice and low parapet with the Royal Arms over the doorway. Simpler arcaded returns and very plain court room block at the rear.

28 Bridge Street, Witney

BRIDGWATER

County Court, Queen Street
Lord Chancellor's Department, Freehold
Grade II*, Group Value, Conservation Area

Early to mid 19th C. An imposing two storey classical facade in Bath stone facing down Court Street and visible from Fore Street. Five bays wide with the centre three breaking forward slightly, columns between windows with Ionic capitals, cornice and pediment. Triple-light sashes to either side with cornice and blocking course over. Pilasters. Segmental-headed ground floor openings with recessed sash windows with glazing bars. Large double doors in opening to the left and a six-panel door up a flight of steps to the right. *UCHB, Pevsner.*

County Court, Bridgwater

ILTON

Wood House Farmhouse, Merryfield
MOD (Navy), Freehold
Grade II

17th C. A substantial two storey farmhouse in stone rubble work. Re-roofed and completely rebuilt internally and with some renewed fenestration. Slate roof with stone slate copings to gable ends. The south front has a two storey gabled porch surmounted by a ball finial. Original two-light mullioned windows with pointed heads to the lights on the first floor with a hood mould over. A hood mould again over the entrance but with carved shield stops. The whole porch is off-centre with one window to the left and two to the right. The rear elevation has two broad gabled wings, largely rebuilt, modern fenestration and entrance. *UCHB.*

Wood House, Farmhouse, Ilton

NORTON FITZWARREN

Norton Manor
MOD (Navy), Freehold
Grade II

Dated 1842 and designed by Henry Roberts for N C Welman. A fine example of Tudor gothic architecture in gault brick with stone quoins and dressings and black brick diapers. Two and a half storeys high with a slate roof. A fine central gabled porch to the main part of the building which itself is well positioned on a terraced steeply falling site, once landscaped but now much overgrown. Many of the original internal features survive including a fine arcaded stair hall and much gothick detailing. *UCHB.*

Stables at Norton Manor, Grade II

Dated 1890, with some of the style of and in similar materials to the manor. In gault brick with stone quoins and dressings and black brick diapering. Built around a courtyard with central tower to the entrance, flanking one and a half storey wings with tiled roofs and grouped octagonal chimneys. The returning wings are generally uninspiring and lacking in character.

Norton Manor, Norton Fitzwarren

PODIMORE

Reedlay House, The Old Rectory
MOD (Navy), Freehold
Grade II

Early 19th C. Two storeys in stucco under a hipped slate roof with a deep soffit. Three window front, sashes with glazing bars, and central doorway with pilasters and entablature. Pilastered quoins and plinth. To the rear, two sash windows vertically, one round-headed sash window to light the stairway, and two dummy windows vertically. *UCHB.*

Reedlay House, Podimore

QUEEN CAMEL

Eyewell House
MOD (Navy), Freehold

C 1926 by Sir Guy Dawber. A pleasant and distinguished house, carefully detailed and well built in a style somewhere between neo-Georgian and the vernacular revival. Two storeys and attic, superbly executed rubble walling. Five windows wide, mainly casements, with segmental arched heads on the ground floor and transoms on the garden front. French windows at ground floor centre with open pediment over. On the entrance facade, to the north, a projecting centre bay in the classical style. At first floor level a sash window with a semi-circular attic window in a steep gable pediment above. Pedimented timber doorcase with panelled reveals and a six-panel door. A massive hipped tiled roof with wide sprocketted eaves, lead dormers and subsidiary roofs linking tremendous chimney stacks on the end walls to the main roof. Single storey annex at the side. Rubble garden walls and dry stone terrace walls in fine grounds. *Pevsner.*

Eyewell House, Queen Camel

WALES FARM HOUSE
MOD (Navy), Freehold
Grade II

Probably early 17th C. Two storeys in coursed rubble with slate roof, coped gables and end brick stacks. Three window frontage with casements in enlarged openings. Central doorway with later addition of Tuscan porch with entablature and blocking course. *UCHB.*

Wales Farm House, Queen Camel

Barn at Wales Farm, Grade II

Probably early 17th C but has undergone some alteration and re-fenestration. In stone rubble. Pitched tiled roof with coped gables and brick chimney stacks.

Pair of Cottages at Wales Farm, Grade II

Probably early 17th C but recently revamped in 20th C rural pastiche. Stone rubble with tiled roof. The original stone chimney stack remains.

TAUNTON

35 East Street
MOD (Army and RAF), Freehold
Grade II, Group Value

Probably mid 19th C. Three storeys in red brick with a parapet. Four bays wide. Modern shop fronts to the ground floor with sash windows above set within recesses with round-headed arches. Second floor sashes with gauged brick flat arches. Dressed stone decoration in the form of an impost band at first floor level, cornice above second floor windows and coping to the brick parapet. *UCHB.*

35 East Street, Taunton

4 Hammet Street
Government Local Offices, Freehold
Grade II*, Group Value, Conservation Area

A terrace of three storey, five window brick fronts dating from 1788–90 when the street was laid out by Sir Benjamin Hammet on the axis of St Mary Magdelene. The properties are divided by plain pilasters terminating in a continuous eaves cornice, above which is a mixture of slate and tile roofs. The rainwater pipes are original. Sash windows, some with glazing bars missing, in plain reveals. Painted stone doorcases with half-round Tuscan pilasters, open pediments and traceried fanlights. Doors with six panels. *UCHB, Pevsner.*

4 Hammet Street, Taunton

TAUNTON

54 Silver Street
Government Offices, Freehold
Grade II

A good 18th C rendered facade. Seven windows, with
stepped lintels, and three storeys high, with later
alterations to the ground floor. Central bay of three
windows breaks forward slightly. Modillion cornice
with centre pediment rising through parapet. Hipped
slate roof. At first floor, sash windows with glazing bars
in timber reveals. Central entrance below with re-
glazed windows to either side and a later porch with an
openwork parapet. Later bay windows to either side,
again with openwork parapet. *UCHB.*

54 Silver Street, Taunton

WELLS

St Cuthbert's Lodge, Chamberlain Street
Government Offices, Hired
Grade II*, Group Value, Conservation Area

Early 18th C. In ashlar, two storeys and an attic. Eight
bays wide with sash windows in bolection moulded
architraves. In the third bay from the left is a moulded
stone doorcase with an open pediment and rectangular fanlight. Plinth, quoins, modillion eaves cornice
and slate roof with four box dormers. Plain outbuild-
ing wing to the left and quadrant walls to a pair of 18th
C stone gate piers with vermiculated rustication,
moulded cornices and large ball finials. *UCHB,
Pevsner.*

YEOVIL

Swallowcliffe, 20 Kingston
Government Offices, Freehold
Grade III

Early 19th C detached stucco house set obliquely to the
road with some later additions. Two storeys, rusticated
quoins and hipped slate roof with deep soffit. A three
window frontage with barred sashes, those at ground
floor level set within arched recesses. Central doorway
with stone Tuscan porch. *UCHB.*

BAGSHOT

Bagshot Park
MOD (Army), Leased
Grade II (central block only)

1877 by Benjamin Ferry for the Duke of Connaught. The estate lies within the Royal Demesne of Windsor, and the present house replaced a Georgian one formerly occupied by the Duke of Gloucester, grandson of Frederick Prince of Wales. The old house, which stood on a low site and had become much dilapidated by the mid 19th C, was demolished shortly before the building of the present house, sited on higher ground to take advantage of the view.

This was the last building by Ferry – a pupil of Pugin and his biographer – and is in an Elizabethan style – very uncharacteristic of one educated in the gothic tradition. It has nothing of the charm and vitality of his earlier church work, which may be due to the fact that Ferry was supposed to have left much of the designing of his later works to his son. There is certainly no great brilliance in this design which relies more on monumentality for its own sake and is archaic for its date. It could easily be mistaken for a building erected 30 years earlier. This may of course have been due to the wishes of the client.

There were five major rooms, supported by labyrinthine service areas, and the whole was planned for later extension – as was duly carried out after Ferry's death in similar style. The interiors are stolid rather than rich or ostentatious, as is usual with Royal Residences. *UCHB, Pevsner, Girouard, The Builder, Country Life*

Bagshot Park, Surrey

CAMBERLEY

The Staff College
MOD (Army), Freehold

The erection of a new building to house the Staff College came at a time of re-organisation of the education of senior officers of the Army. The Crimean War had shown up deficiencies in the staff, and a programme of improvement in military officers was initiated. The Duke of Cambridge, appointed Commander in Chief in 1856, immediately interested himself in educational questions with the result that the Senior Department of the Royal Military College was re-named 'Staff College.' Previously the education and qualification of officers had been a rather haphazard affair, now a proper course with a new syllabus was initiated and new premises were required.

In 1858 James Pennethorne, Surveyor to the Office of Works, was asked to submit plans for a new college building. Pennethorne had been the architect for the completion of Somerset House after the death of Sir William Chambers. The design for the new building has certain affinity with the 'New Wing' of the latter, but is rather more severe and was at the time an almost unique concept of a large purpose built accommodation and teaching block.

Building started in 1859 and was completed in 1862. The building operations were directly responsible for the establishment of 'Cambridge Town' along the main road adjacent to the site. This later became the Camberley of to-day.

The building is a highly impressive and articulate design, very finely detailed. It originally provided accommodation for 40 officers, with Mess Room and Ante-Room.

The interiors are rather plain and business-like save for the Entrance Hall, which is a superb example of Pennethorne's mastery of space manipulation for grand effect. It rises through the full height of the building, top lit and in a variety of stones. There is no grand central stair as one might have expected, the ingenious staircase is to one side behind the flank wall of the Hall, but is no less magnificent being all of Cragleith stone, and leads up to a gallery with wrought iron balustrades. It has since had added a large memorial of 1888 in marble and alabaster, and a Great War memorial of blue and brown Hornton stone. Although both these have been carefully placed they do detract somewhat from Pennethorne's original concept of large opulent space with carefully articulated superimposed orders.

There were originally spiral staircases at each end of the building which have since been replaced by bathroom towers. Between 1910 and 1913 a third storey was added, increasing the French appearance of the building, the mess room was considerably enlarged and a billiard room and library constructed in the lightwells. The latter has its original joinery and stained glass and is a very good example of Edwardian interior decoration which has survived well. *Pevsner.*

Staff College, Camberley

CATERHAM

Guards Depot Chapel, Coulsdon Road
MOD (Army), Freehold

1881 by William Butterfield, yellow stock brick with Bath stone dressings and minimal purple brick decoration. Except for some knapped flint work mainly at high level the polychromy is as restrained as the rest of the depot buildings, begun in 1877. Curious rounded detail on the lower parts of the buttresses. Steeply pitched tiled roofs.

The interior has the low breadth characteristic of garrison churches. Aisled nave of four generous bays, the westernmost pair of supports being wide piers balancing the chancel walls. The arcade sup-

ports retain their polychromy of alternate courses of buff limestone and red sandstone but the arches have been rendered. Twin windows in the west wall separated by an internal buttress supporting the bellcote. Panelled timber roof on substantial arched trusses. The low narrow south aisle with a beam to roof contrasts with the taller, wider flat ceilinged north aisle. Two bay chancel flanked by a side chapel and the organ chamber. The only architectural division above floor level between nave and chancel is a double roof truss with pierced spandrel infill supporting a Rood. Fine encaustic tile sanctuary floor. *Pevsner.*

FARNHAM   *Southern*

18 West Street
Manpower Services Commission, Leased
Grade II, Group Value, Conservation Area

A three storey early 19th C red brick house with a

front of three unequal bays, the centre one slightly recessed; hipped slate roof. The ground floor and lower half of the first floor have been wiped out by a modern shop front, with a vehicular passage in the left hand bay. *UCHB.*

FRIMLEY

Mytchett Place
MOD (Army), Freehold

1779. Built for a Mrs Willis to replace an earlier farmhouse, the building occupied the area now covered by part of the kitchens, dining room, drawing room and main hall. The building was then known as Mytchett House. In 1795 it was changed to Hollest Place, and in 1823 re-named Mytchett Lodge. It was not until 1882 that the present name of Mytchett Place was given it. At this date the building ceased being a farmhouse and became purely a 'Gentleman's residence,' the gentleman being a Mr George James Murray.

As befits a gentleman, he considerably enlarged and altered the house adding the study, front hall, porch, kitchens, billiard room, and the curious tower (now derelict).

The building is well sited overlooking a terraced garden and has an imposing appearance. It is of brick construction throughout, stuccoed to give an Italianate air. The entrance hall and staircase is impressive, panelled with the stairwell top lit and rising to an arcaded top landing. The principal rooms are now all used as offices, and the finest

Mytchett Place, Frimley

room – the dining room – has been partitioned across. There is still some good surviving joinery, ironmongery and fireplaces.

The house was purchased by the War Department in 1912 and it was used until 1960 as a residence. During the 1940's Rudolf Hess was imprisoned here for two years.

There is a stable block, mid Victorian and converted, and a picturesque gate lodge.

GODALMING

16 High Street
Manpower Services Commission. Freehold
Grade II, Group Value, Conservation Area

An 18th C three storey red brick house with a three
window front, with keystones to sash windows,
ornamental brick eaves and tiled mansard roof with
hipped ends. 19th C shop front. At the east end of
the important group forming the main part of the
High Street. *UCHB.*

16 High Street, Godalming

HEADLEY

Headley Court, Surrey

Headley Court, RAF Headley Court
MOD (RAF), Leased

A large Edwardian country house in Jacobean style,
by Edward P Warren for Walter, First Baron Cun-
liffe, incorporating the remains of a small farmhouse and built on the foundations of a very large
mansion of which no record survives. Two storeys
and attic on an irregular but well organised L-
shaped plan. Red brick with stone mullion and
transom windows and square, canted and semi-
circular bays including some first floor oriels. Tiled
roofs with a plethora of Dutch gables and hip-
roofed dormers.

The interior is more remarkable with a great variety of 17th C wooden panelling rescued from demolished buildings, including the earlier house on
the site, and new woodwork of high quality. The
former drawing room, now the ante-room, has a
very fine Jacobean style plaster ceiling by Lawrence
Turner.

Set in beautiful and immaculately maintained
grounds on the northern slopes of the North Downs
with a splendid view across the Thames Valley. At
the end of the northern axis is a large ornamental
basin also intended as a bathing place.

Early in World War II Headley Court was requisitioned as a Canadian Forces Headquarters. After
the war it was purchased by the Trustees of the
Royal Air Force Pilots and Crews Fund, raised as a
memorial by the Chartered Auctioneers and Estate
Agents Institute, and leased to the RAF as a rehabi-
litation centre. Fortunately the buildings erected
subsequently have harmonised well with the original
and respected the layout of the grounds. *Pevsner,
Country Life.*

LONG CROSS

Barrowhills
MOD (Procurement Executive), Freehold

1852–53 by William Wilmer Pocock as his own summer residence. He succeeded to the large practice of his father W F Pocock, an unremarkable architect, but astute surveyor and author of several architectural books. W W Pocock bought the estate of nearly 100 acres with an existing keeper's cottage already on the site.

There was also a barn, stables and a farmyard. During the summer months the family occupied the cottage on their visits, Pocock having rebuilt the stables with accommodation for the keeper's family above – this still remains though largely derelict. He then built a small bailiff's cottage in order that he and his family might occupy the existing cottage in winter if they required, but this being too near the farmyard for comfort Pocock decided to build himself a new house on higher ground.

"I soon set to work to make bricks and tiles, burning them with wood cut down on the spot, and built a decent sized house . . ." He called the house 'Three Barrows'. A picture of this rather bijou villa in Victorian rustic Surrey vernacular style exists in the present house. Pocock eventually sold the house and the estate being unsatisfied with the quality of religious services offered in the neighbourhood and as his wife thought the house and its size of rooms too large. Also he needed the money for housing developments in London which were an important part of the practice.

The house eventually passed to Sir John Mullins in 1907 who made extensive alterations to form the house of today. These were principally the addition of a range of four large bay windowed reception rooms, with further bedrooms above, which more than doubled the size of the house. (Plans for these works are kept at the house, and show the work as being carried out by J W Heath and Son Builders of Cromwell Road, London). Sir John Mullins sold the property in 1920 to Lord Camrose, who added the swimming pool but mercifully seems to have left the earlier alterations. Subsequently the property deteriorated, its low point coming with its purchase in 1952 by the Ministry of Supply from St George's College Preparatory School. The school was allowed to remove everything portable or removable including ornamental garden furniture, clocks, crystal chandeliers from the balloon and even the name board, which they took with them to their new premises at Witley, Godalming. Fortunately, there is much remaining which is of importance – the fine Art Nouveau door furniture, the chimney pieces, the smoking room joinery and the dining room buffet. There is even a tiled bathroom remianing upstairs, and some very fine panelling and carved staircase in the entrance hall. The dining room ingle-nook looks into a charming grotto-like aviary built into the south front, and there is a delightful path through the wood behind the house with a rockery and cascade falling intor a formal pool with foot bridge, on the terrace. The house is now the Military Vehicles Experimental Establishment Officers' Mess and, is in fine order and well suited to its new role.

Barrowhills, Long Cross

WEST BYFLEET

Broadoaks
Ministry of Defence, Freehold

1876, architect Ernest Seth Smith, for his elder brother, Charles.

The house was built on the site of Shepherd's Farmhouse, part of which was incorporated in the ground floor of the new house. Numerous outbuildings were also retained. At the turn of the century the property was acquired by Sir Charles Tennant who let it to Major Collis Browne, who made extensive alterations and additions. In 1911 the estate was bought by the Charrington family who enlarged and altered the house further.

The house now has a pleasant rambling look to it which is so indicative of accretions over the years. Unfortunately recent developments have ruined its aspect and the surrounding pleasure gardens have completely disappeared.

The main entrance is most unspectacular and opens into a very small vestibule with the rather insignificant staircase off one side. Fortunately there is still a wealth of superb interior decorations and fittings which have survived well despite unsuitable use. The ballroom is probably the grandest room with a vaulted ceiling and elaborate ribs and pendants. The main conference room (originally the boudoir) has decorated gilt panelling and there are many more interesting details to be found around the house.

Broadoaks, West Byfleet

The outbuildings still attached to the estate include lodges and cottages and a most unusual covered tennis court, now a garage. There is also a charming model dairy and a pump-house adjacent to the reservoir in a totally ruinous state. Two little timber summerhouses also survive.

The property was purchased by the Ministry of supply in 1946 and the careless planning of new buildings since the war has ruined the delight aspect and prospect of the site.

Broadoaks, West Byfleet

WORPLESDON

Tangley Place, Worplesdon

Tangley Place
Ministry of Agriculture, Freehold

C1885–1900? A complete enigma of a house, historically. This large Tudor style building of some pretension gives the appearance of an architectural hybrid, and rather clumsily articulated. It was apparently connected in the early years of the century with the Wills tobacco family, later passing to the Judewine family in the 1920's. It is now the Worplesdon Laboratory of the Ministry of Agriculture, Fisheries and Food.

Nothing remains of its once extensive grounds which included a sunken garden and lily pond, and the interiors have been thoroughly decimated by insensitive decoration schemes, partitions and general use as offices and laboratories. Examples of the previous grandeur of the house are found occasionally. Fine doors and door cases, panelling congealed with paintwork, a good fitted library, elaborately tiled bathroom and a very good chimney piece boxed-in for protection – in what was once the drawing room. A house that would repay greater research.

Tangley Place, Worplesdon

ARDINGLY

WAKEHURST PLACE
Ministry of Agriculture, Leased
Grade I

Wakehurst Place, Ardingly

As originally built for Sir Edward Culpeper in 1590 the present main body of the house was the north range of a much larger courtyard house. The south range was demolished before 1697 and the east and west wings shortened by two thirds in 1848, their original ends being rebuilt.

The house was greatly altered in the early 1870s for Lady Downshire. The entrance and staircase were moved, the principal rooms extended into the east wing and a replacement kitchen and offices provided in the new north west wing and the chapel built onto the north east. In the 1890s it was further restored by Sir Aston Webb, who built the north porch for Lord Wakefield in 1903. Further restoration took place in 1938 when the upper part of the south front was rebuilt.

Two storeys and attic, of Wealden sandstone with a Horsham stone roof. The main south front is a most satisfying composition with generous mullion and transom windows, the upper lights of which have three-centred heads, a most conservative feature for their date. The projecting porch has a frontispiece of superimposed Doric and Ionic col-

umns with a steeply pitched pediment. The roof breaks out in a plethora of pinnacled gables and dormers. The north, entrance front is effectively Victorian.

The interior has fine plaster ceilings, chimney pieces, staircases and screens of various periods, much of it repositioned. *UCHB, Pevsner, G Loder 'History of Wakehurst Place', Connoisseur.*

Stables at Wakehurst Place

212

ARDINGLY

Stable at Wakehurst Place, Grade II

Early 18th C two storey Wealden sandstone ashlar block. Five bay show front facing the north side of the house across the entrance court, the wide centre bay broken forward and pedimented. Plinth, rusticated quoins and first floor band course, moulded cornice and parapet. Segmental headed windows and arched doorway. Hipped Horsham stone roof. The front was rebuilt from the ground and the octagonal timber cupola renewed in 1938 when the matching block to the north and low link to the west were built.

Wakehurst Place was left to the National Trust in 1963 by Sir Henry Price and leased as an outstation of the Royal Botanic Gardens, Kew in 1965. The gardens and parts of the ground floor of the house are open to the public throughout the year.

CHICHESTER

44 North Street
Ministry of Agriculture, Hired
Grade II, Group Value, Conservation Area

18th C three storey red brick house, painted five window front, flush sash windows with glazing bars. Off-centre doorcase with attached Doric columns, entablature blocks and open pediment. Panelled reveals to semi-circular headed doorway with traceried fanlight and six-panel door. Brick dentil eaves cornice to hipped tile roof. *UCHB.*

52 North Street
MOD (Army), Freehold
Grade II, Group Value, Conservation Area

Elegant early 19th C painted stucco five window front. Doorway with Greek Doric columns in antis and entablature with first floor sill level band course

52, North Street, Chichester

forming blocking course. Six-panel door. Shouldered architrave surrounds to first floor windows, the centre one with a cornice. Moulded cornice and low parapet; hipped slate roof.

WISTON

Wiston House
Foreign Office, Hired
Grade I

Built for Sir Thomas Shirley after he was knighted in 1573 but drastically rebuilt c 1830 by Edward Blore for Charles Goring so that only the east entrance front is original, its fine pale ashlar easily distinguishable from Blore's ashlar dressed squared rubble. The entrance court was formally fully enclosed but now makes an E-shaped front. The three storey centre has immense mullion and transom windows rising through the double height of the hall on the left of the porch matched by identical windows masking two floors on the right. The porch is pedimented above superimposed orders of paired pilasters. The cornice and parapet above with its terminal volutes are 18th C. The wings are two storeyed with shaped gables.

Blore's elevations are substantial rather than inspiring. Built into the west side is a large 16th C fireplace of uncertain provenance. The interior is largely Blore's with much imported panelling though the former dining room has its original panelling dated 1576. The great hall has a feeble hammer beam roof but magnificent stucco wall decoration including a rococo gothic fireplace, niches and doorways. *UCHB, Pevsner.*

ABLINGTON

Ablington, Wiltshire

MOD (Army), Freehold

A pleasing hamlet of whitewashed and thatched cottages (one dated 1665), all of which have been modernised in more recent times and are in an excellent state of repair. A great deal of attention has also been paid to the boundary fences, gates and hedges.

Syrencot House
Grade II

Mid 18th C. Three storeys in vitreous brick with red dressings. Stone plinth, quoins and strings at floor levels. Dentil cornice and blocking course with hipped slate roof behind. East front of five bays, the centre first floor window being arched and the remainder segmental-headed, but all with stone keystones. To the right, a lower two storey extension, again in vitreous and red brick, but with irregular early 19th C casement windows. Six-panel door with eared architrave surround under a Doric portico, entablature with triglyph frieze, to the left of the wing and adjoining the main house. Prior to the D-Day landings in June 1944 Syrencot House was the headquarters of the First and Sixth Airborne Divisions, the troops of which played a vital part in the successful assault on mainland Europe. *UCHB, Pevsner.*

Syrencot House, Ablington

BULFORD

St George's Garrison Church
MOD (Army), Freehold

1920-27 by GLW Blount and Williamson. In coursed rubble with ashlar dressings. Basically cruciform in plan, but with aisles to north and south and with a tower over the crossing. Five light aisle windows and rose windows to the north, south and west. Slate roof. *Pevsner.*

St George, Bulford

CHIPPENHAM

23-24 Market Place
Government Offices, Leased
Grade II, Group Value

No 23, formerly a Burgage house and largely rebuilt after 1835. No 24 dating from the late 18th C, was also rebuilt at the same time being formerly the Lamb public house. Three storeys in height with two windows to No 24 and three to No 23, the latter having a splayed corner treatment. Hipped Welsh slate roof with former stacks removed. Limestone ashlar with the face of No 23 rebuilt and rendered. No 24 has plain first floor banding and plinth. Both buildings with recessed sash windows. At ground floor level No 23 has a modern shop front inserted but No 24 still has the original round-arched doorway with edge rolls, radial fan light and panelled door. *UCHB.*

CHITTERNE

Chitterne Farm
MOD (Army), Freehold
Grade III

Early 19th C with later alterations. In brick, two storeys high with part slate and part pantile roof. L-shaped on plan. Three casement windows to the first floor. Central door with flat hood on cut brackets, flanked by 19th C angular stone bay windows. *UCHB.*

Flint Cottage
MOD (Army), Freehold

19th C. Two storeys in stone with brick quoins and surrounds to openings. Three bays, sash windows and central door with canopy over. Pitched slate roof with brick chimney stacks at each gable end.

Chitterne Farm, Wiltshire

Flint Cottage, Chitterne

CHITTERNE

Brook Cottage, Chitterne

Manor Farm, Chitterne

Brook Cottage
MOD (Army), Freehold

Probably 18th C. Two storeys in stone and flint chequer. Pantiled roof with brick chimney stacks at gable ends. Three windows and central door with tiled porch. Sensitive single storey extension to the left.

Manor Farm
MOD (Army), Freehold

A large 19th C building. Two storeys in banded ashlar and flint with pantiled roof. Three bays. Ground floor windows with dressed stone mullions and transoms with hood moulds over. Steps up to six-panelled front door set within a revival version of a five-centred arch. Stone porch hood on corbels. Casement windows above with stone mullions only and breaking the eaves line. Gables with coped verges over each window. A well maintained building surrounded by a fine garden.

DEVIZES

Cromwell House, 31 Market Place
Ministry of Agriculture, Freehold
Grade II, Group Value, Conservation Area

Early 19th C. Formerly the Cromwell Hotel. Three storeys and basement in painted stucco with banding at first floor sill level. Moulded cornice and blocking course. Slate roof. Four bays with multi-paned sash windows to first and second floors but with three windows at ground floor level and two in the basement. Contemporary flanking cast iron plain rails and scrapers to four stone steps leading from the pavement up to the main entrance on the right of centre. Six-panel double doors in an arched recess with moulded capitals at the springing of the arch. Arched fanlight over with curved glazing, struck from different centres, together with the original lantern. *UCHB.*

Cromwell House, Devizes

DURRINGTON

Red House, High Street
Property Services Agency, Freehold
Grade III

Early 19th C. Two storeys in red brick and five bays
wide. Sash windows with glazing bars in square
headed openings, gauged brick flat arches. Central
doorway with portico on Doric columns. Overhanging hipped slate roof. Brick chimney stack. *UCHB.*

Red House, Durrington

EAST CHISENBURY

Cottages 508, 512 and 533
MOD (Army), Freehold
Grade III

Three out of a group of five traditional cottages
situated between the road and the old mill race.
Cottage 508 dates from 18th C, two storeys in red
brick under a thatched roof. Irregular and recently
modernised although not unsuccessfully. Cottage
512 is again two storeys in height but timber
framed with brick infill panels. Plaster infilling to
the east front and brick to the west. Thatched roof.
Cottage 533 is 17th C, two storeys in chalk with
brick dressings, again with a thatched roof. *UCHB.*

Cottage 508, East Chisenbury

Cottage 512, East Chisenbury

ENFORD

Baden Farm House
MOD (Army), Freehold

A long low two storey farmhouse under a thatched roof with hipped gables. The older part of the building undoubtedly being the central half-timbered portion into which windows have been inserted at different architectural periods over the years. To either end, later additions or extensions in redbrick or a combination of red and vitreous brick.

Boden Farmhouse, Enford

Lower Enford Farm House

Cottage at Compton, Wiltshire

9, 10 Long Street
MOD (Army), Freehold
Grade III

Early 19th C. Two storeys. Flint and coursed rubble in bands with brick dressings and base. Thatched roof. Four two-light and one three-light casement window with two doorways at ground floor level. There is a two storey extension under a tiled roof to the left. *UCHB.*

9, 10 Long Street, Enford

Lower Enford Farmhouse
MOD (Army), Freehold

Georgian. Brick and flint facade. Two storeys, three bays with multi-paned sash windows. At ground floor level a central doorway, with contemporary porch over, flanked by windows with gauged brick flat arches. Over all a hipped slate roof with brick chimney stacks at either end.

Cottage on the A345, near Compton
MOD (Army), Freehold

A pleasing single storey thatched cottage, with attic, in coursed stone and brickwork now whitewashed. A more recent extension to the left has been well handled giving the building an almost symmetrical elevation about a gable with attic window above the main entrance.

FIFIELD

Fifield Farmhouse
MOD (Army), Freehold
Grade III

17th C. Two storeys, part flint and brick, part brick, all colour washed with sham timber framing painted on. Hipped thatched roof. A long irregular west front, the left-hand part single storey, with a modern lattice porch under a thatched roof in the second bay from the right beneath a single casement. The lower part to the left is irregular. A south front of three bays with early 19th C casement windows and a half glazed central door in timber Greek Doric porch. *UCHB*.

Fifield Farmhouse, Wiltshire

FIGHELDEAN

Cottage 305
MOD (Army), Freehold

One of a row of three cottages in a variety of materials including timber framing with wattle and daub infilling, and walls of stone, chalk and brick, now for the main part rendered over and painted. Basically single storey with attic accommodation over resulting in dormer lights, gable ends and othe roof features designed to tax the thatcher's skill to the utmost.

Cottage 305, Figheldean

FITTLETON

Haxton Farm, Haxton
MOD (Army), Freehold
Grade II

Late 18th C. Two storeys in brick with red brick quoins, window surrounds and bands, all framing vitreous brick panels. Later colour washed but now wearing off. Dentil first floor string. Old tile roof. The facade to the east is of five bays with a six-panel central door, the upper panels glazed, in a stone Doric doorcase. The house is approached from the east by a fine avenue of lime trees. *UCHB*.

Haxton Farm, Fittleton

HULLAVINGTON

Two barns, RAF Hullavington
MOD (RAF), Freehold
Grade II

Barn at RAF Hullavington

17th C. Formerly part of Bell Farm which itself was demolished in 1936 to make way for the new aerodrome. Both barns are constructed in stone rubble and have stone tile roofs. One barn is approximately 65' by 25' with cart doors both sides and a porch on the farmyard side; unfortunately one of the cart doors has been bricked up somewhat unsympathetically. A five-bay roof with simple trussed principals. The other barn is approximately 70' by 20' with a cart door and porch only on the farm yard side. A 6 to 7 bay roof with trussed principals. *UCHB*.

IMBER

MOD (Army), Freehold

This remote village in the heart of Salisbury Plain was purchased by the Army c 1930. It was evacuated in 1943 when the artillery ranges were extended for intensive training prior to D-Day and has remained unoccupied since then. Little remains of the original village save a few buildings including the Bell Inn, Imber Court and St Giles's Church, of which only the last is intact.

St Giles's Church

13th C in origin, on a simple plan with nave and aisles, north porch and a western tower of c 1380. The chancel was built in 1849. The late Saxon/early Norman font together with two stone effigies and the five bells from the tower have been removed for safe keeping. The effigies can be seen in Edington Church to the north of Salisbury Plain. *Pevsner*.

St Giles, Imber

LARKHILL

St Alban's Garrison Church, The Packway
MOD (Army), Freehold

1937 by W A Ross, who was then chief architect to the War Office. A large imposing structure in red brick. Low tower to south west. Tall and narrow windows with pointed arches set within reveals between brick buttresses. Polygonal apse. Brick interior with low aisle-passages. *Pevsner*.

St Alban, Larkhill

LITTLE CHEVERELL

Manor Farm
MOD (Army), Freehold

18th C. Two storey three bay rendered facade with continuous sill moulding at first floor level. At ground floor a central doorway beneath a 19th C timber porch with tiled roof and flanked by multi-paned sash windows. Three similar windows above but with the one in the centre being slightly narrower that the other two. Parapet and coping adorned with two fir cone finials, one at either end. Tiled roof with brick chimney stacks flanking the gables at either end. To the north west is a large 19th C two storey brick extension with a tiled roof. An interesting tile-clad first floor bay is supported on delicate cast iron columns.

Manor Farm, Little Cheverell

LITTLECOTT

Littlecott Farm House
MOD (Army), Freehold

19th C, in painted brickwork. Constructed length-ways along the contours of a steeply sloping site with two storeys to the north east entrance facade and three to the south west facing across the valley. Hipped slate roof with brick chimney stacks. The house has undergone considerable alteration and extension during its lifetime but this has only been sympathetically handled on the north east side of the building where an attempt has been made to harmonise with the original fenestration and overall scale.

Little Farm House, Wiltshire

LUDGERSHALL

Castle Farm House, Castle Street
MOD (Army), Freehold
Grade III, Conservation Area

Late 18th C. Two storeys in brick, under an old tile roof. A three bay south front with mid 19th C sash windows and a central gabled glazed porch. *UCHB.*

Castle Farm House, Ludgershall

MELKSHAM

New Hall, Market Place
Manpower Services Commission, Lease

Dated 1877. Ashlar, in the classical style. Three bays defined by Doric pilasters rising from a deep plinth. Banding above and pediment with escutcheon containing the letters 'BP' and the date. Round-headed sash windows grouped two per round-headed and recessed bay. Flanking narrow pilasters and floral motif in the tympanum. Heavy central projecting porch again with Doric pilasters. Entablature engraved 'New Hall', with cornice and blocking course over, the whole feature obliterating the lower part of the fenestration to the central bay.

New Hall, Melksham

NETHERAVON

Outbuildings at Manor Farm
MOD (Army), Freehold
Grade III

An immense courtyard group of barns and outbuildings to the west of the house in weatherboard and thatch. *UCHB*.

Netheravon Stable Block
MOD (Army), Freehold
Grade II, Conservation Area

Late 18th C, a large courtyard block to the north west of the house, to which it is linked by a curved colonnade. Red brick with hipped slate roofs, the elevations treated as pilastered arcades with semi-elliptical and semi-circular windows and a splendid elliptical window beneath the pediment on the east side. It has suffered by the insertion of unsympathetic modern windows.

Netheravon Dovecote
MOD (Army), Freehold
Ancient Monument, Grade II, Conservation Area

Square on plan, red brick with brick dentil eaves cornice, hipped slate tiled roof with louvred dormers and central turret.

Dovecote, Netheravon

Wexland Farm
MOD (Army), Freehold
Grade III

18th C, but it has undergone much alteration. Brickwork with rendered quoins. Two storeys and attic under a hipped tiled roof with flanking chimneys. Three dormer windows to the south facade with five bays of modern windows and a modern central door. To the front is a terraced garden with a central gate. *UCHB*.

RUDLOE

Rudloe Manor, Wiltshire

RUDLOE MANOR
MOD (RAF), Freehold
Grade II

C 1685 and built by Thomas Goddard. Two storeys with attic in stone and rubble. Four bays each with three-light stone mullion windows with continuous hood moulds and bearing arches and small centrally placed oval windows. Moulded stone eaves cornice with a large hipped stone roof above including two hipped dormers. Central stone chimney with diagonal stacks. Some restoration to the rear, but despite this a few medieval windows remain. *UCHB, Pevsner.*

Cart Shed at Rudloe Manor

Cart Shed at Rudloe Manor

Barn at Rudloe Manor, Grade II

A medieval barn adjacent to the manor with two buttresses on the south side. Original roof timbers but retiled during recent conversion to office use.

With the former two buildings makes an interesting group about the forecourt. Almost certainly 19th C but with a fine stone roof and some interesting roof trusses. Eight bays, open to the east with massive circular columns in coursed rubble.

SALISBURY

Rougemont, London Road
Government Offices, Freehold

Early 20th C, a large double fronted house of two storeys and attic. Mainly in red brick with decorative horizontal banding and some ashlar detailing around the central doorway and above the windows. Gable ends incorporating sham half-timbered effect. Slate roof with squat brick chimney stacks. To the rear are various outbuildings including a stable block, now converted to garages.

Rougemont, Salisbury

Cross Keys House, Queen Street
Manpower Services Commission, Part Hired
Conservation Area

1878 by H Hall. Two storeys plus attic in gothic style.

Ground floor of red brick with ashlar plinth banding, mullion and transom window, and surround to door. Sham timber framing and infill panels to first floor as well as some ground floor detailing repeated. Gable ended attic window, tiled roof with a small gable ended dormer light and tall square brick chimney stack.

TILSHEAD

The Elms
MOD (Army), Freehold

17th C. A much altered and extended cottage, the right hand half of which is basically constructed in flint and chalk blocks. Interesting features include stone mullioned windows, with hood moulds, to the rear elevation. In the early 20th C the roof was removed and the walls raised to provide two storey accommodation, with a similar extension to the east in brickwork but all now under a hipped tiled roof. This was followed almost immediately by another extension to the south. Despite its somewhat tortuous development the house is not without character.

The Elms, Tilshead

TROWBRIDGE

5 Fore Street
Lord Chancellor's Department, Hired
Grade II, Group Value, Conservation Area

C 1864 and formerly part of Salter's offices. Ornately Italian in style. Three storeys high in ashlar and seven window elevation. Flanking pilasters. Rusticated ground floor with vermiculated bases and quoins to end pilasters and former wide openings, now shop fronts. Tall doorway to the left with segmental head and door with six raised and fielded panels. Dentil cornice over. Round headed first floor windows with wide surrounds, keys and beaded edges to spandrels separated by pilasters with cross-hatched capitals. Moulded band over the first floor with a panel containing 'Samuel Salter & Co' in raised letters and with carved panels on pilasters at either end. Plate glass sash windows with shouldered lintels to second floor, with carved rinceaux to moulded reveals, palmette imposts and plain keystones. Continuous moulded banding above the windows. Modillion cornice and blocking course. The rear is of red brick with an ashlar ground floor, ashlar banding, grey brick dressings and quoins. Round-headed first floor windows with cast iron glazing bars. Shouldered lintels to second floor windows with projecting box eaves over. *UCHB.*

Homefield House, Trowbridge

8 Fore Street
Government Offices, Hired
Grade II, Group Value, Conservation Area

With No 7, probably mid 18th C. Two storeys with attic, ashlar fronted and framed by draughted pier strips. No 7 is three bays wide and No 8 five, all with glazing bar sash windows within moulded architrave aprons at first floor level. Moulded eaves cornice with pier breaks. New tiled roof and dormer lights, one to No 7 and two to No 8. Gable end chimneys, off the ridge to the right. No 8 has a 20th C five bay extension of No 7's Doric entablature, supported by dividing pilasters, but improved by triglyphs and guttae. The left hand bay is a doorway. *UCHB.*

Homefield House, Polebarn Road
Government Offices, Freehold
Grade II*, Group Value, Conservation Area

With Rosefield House, a late 18th or early 19th C pair of houses. Three storeys to the road in Bath stone on a projecting plinth. Rusticated ground floor treatment. Plain string at first floor sill level and carved string with diaper pattern at second floor sill level. Over all a plain frieze with moulded cornice and parapet with balustraded panels over the windows. The front is divided into four bays by slightly projecting pilasters which run the whole height of the facade and are decorated with an incised key pattern. Glazing bars to the sash windows, within slight recesses with segmental heads on the ground floor. The entry to Rosefield House is in the second bay from the left. A half glazed door with reeded lower panels and a rectangular fanlight with curved and radiating pattern. A stone porch with two pairs of slender piers, incised key pattern, supporting a panelled architrave carved with key fret and diamonds over the piers and a small balustrade with angle blocks enriched with fan motifs. Small arched heads to side openings and a three-centred arch supported on small offsets to the piers over the central entrance. The design is reminiscent of Sir John Soane's work.

The entry to Homefield House is now in a large three storey 1950's extension of one plus six windows in a sympathetic style which retains a two storey bow on the south east return of the main house. A bow also on the north west end which has small cast iron flower guards. Two pairs of cast iron panelled gate standards of diagonal pattern with urn finials to the road. Small wrought iron gate to Homefield House. One remaining rusticated stone pier with key pattern at base of capping. *UCHB, Pevsner.*

UPTON SCUDAMORE

Cottage No 33
MOD (Army), Freehold
Grade II

Dated 1723 on stone over the door. Two storeys in brick with stone quoins on a moulded stone plinth and with a moulded stone string at first floor level. Old tiled roof with stone eaves cornice. Symmetrical elevation to the road with two three-light moulded stone mullioned casement windows to each floor with a central four-panel door in moulded stone surround and an altered flat wooden hood over. Wing to rear similar but with the door altered. *UCHB, Pevsner.*

Cottage 33, Upton Scudamore

WARMINSTER

Milestone at Parsonage Farm, Elm Hill
MOD (Army), Freehold
Grade II

Dated 1840 with the makers' plate (Carson and Miller of Warminster) C & M over W, 1840. Cast iron with moulded pyramidal capping and raised lettering. Set against a farmyard well. Legend reads 'Warminster Town Hall 1 mile, Bratton 5 miles'. One of several such in Warminster. *UCHB.*

WEST CHISENBURY

West Chisenbury Farm
MOD (Army), Freehold

C 1900, a pleasing two storey brick farmhouse, L-shaped on plan, with plinth and deep first floor sill banding in the same material. Later hipped tiled roof with brick chimney stacks. Pleasantly proportioned sash windows with segmental brick arches over. To the right is a single bay projection at ground floor level with a stone coping and ball finial decoration. Round-headed opening to porchway.

West Chisenbury Farm, Wiltshire

WESTBURY

LEIGHTON HOUSE, Warminster Road
MOD (Army), Freehold
Grade II

Leighton House, Westbury

1800, but thoroughly altered and extended in 1888. The original part of the building is three storeys high. In ashlar with a rusticated ground floor and modillion cornice with astragal and blocking course. Five bays, with the central bay breaking forward slightly to form a backing for a portico porch. Late glazed sashes, square on the second floor. The first floor window over the portico has three lights. Projecting Roman Doric tetrastyle portico, now glazed in, with full Doric frieze, cornice and blocking course. The glazing contains good painted panels of figures and animals. Fine hanging cast iron lantern. Central entrance with low relief pediment in the lintel.

The late 19th C additions and alterations by Frank Willis of Bristol include a two-bay wing in matching style to the east and a large conservatory, six bays by four, to the west. The latter with panelled parapet, raised skylight with painted glass sides, and wide arched windows with painted glass in the spandrels; a smaller arched entrance to the right with keyed oculus over. Various extensions to the rear also in ashlar and dating from the 19th C. One rear chimney has a shield with the Laverton arms and motto; the arms also occur on several cast iron rainwater hoppers. One lead rainwater hopper supports the date 1800 and the initials of the original owner Thomas Henry Mele

Phipps. The interior of the house was also refurbished by Frank Willis; there is a fine large hall with a two-column screen to a wide staircase which has a very ornate acanthus balustrade. *UCHB.*

Stable block at Leighton House, Grade II

C 1800 but has undergone some alteration. A three sided stable court, approached from Leighton House by a bridge over Warminster Road. In ashlar, two storeys in the centre and five bays wide. A central gabled break with sharply angled modillions and inset clock. Below, a two storey archway (now blocked) with moulded architrave and coat of arms within the tympanum. Belfry over added in the late 19th C. To each side of this central break are two glazing bar sash windows on the upper floors and two segmental headed three-light glazing bar casements below. The ground floor is protected by a glass lean-to. Hipped slate roof with two ridge chimneys, Two single flanking wings of five bays each, slightly lower than the central block and with large hospital-type bar sashes. The tie rings for tethering horses are still in place. A low closing wall to the south west.

**Gate piers and side gates at Leighton House
Grade II**

C 1800 but altered and adapted. Tall outer gate piers linked by quadrant walls to four tall inner gate piers. All stone with moulded capping and ball finials. Massive and ornately decorative cast iron side gates with lamp overthrow, probably post 1888 for W H Laverton. The main gates have been lost but the flat overthrow remains now incorporates a 20th C panel capped by a crown. Plaques from the original bridge which connected Leighton House to the stables are set in the quadrant walls – large stone shields with the Phipps arms. Stone walls on each side ramped up to the outer piers. Within and adjacent to the entrance gates is a small lodge, which although not listed is not without character.

Stables at Leighton House, Westbury   *Gates at Leighton House, Westbury*